THE FOUNDERS' KEY

The Divine and Natural Connection
Between the Declaration and the Constitution
and What We Risk by Losing It

Larry P. Arnn

THOMAS NELSON
Since 1798

NASHVILLE   DALLAS   MEXICO CITY   RIO DE JANEIRO

Published in Nashville, Tennessee, by Thomas Nelson. Thomas Nelson is a registered trademark of Thomas Nelson, Inc.

Thomas Nelson, Inc., titles may be purchased in bulk for educational, business, fund-raising, or sales promotional use. For information, please e-mail SpecialMarkets@ThomasNelson.com.

Library of Congress Cataloging-in-Publication Data
Arnn, Larry P., 1952-
  The founders' key : the divine and natural connection between the Declaration and the Constitution and what we risk by losing it / Larry P. Arnn.
    p. cm.
  Includes bibliographical references.
  ISBN 978-1-59555-472-7
  1. United States—Politics and government. 2. Natural law—Religious aspects. 3. United States. Declaration of Independence. 4. United States. Constitution. 5. Constitutional law—United States—Religious aspects. I. Title.
  JK31.A76 2012
  320.101—dc23

                                                                    2011041283

Printed in the United States of America

13 14 15 16 17 RRD 12 11 10 9 8

To Penny and our children,
Katy, Henry, Alice, and Tony

Contents

PART I:
THE ARGUMENT

~⌐ ONE ⌐~

ETERNAL, YET NEW

The second day of July, 1776, will be the most memorable epoch in the history of America. I am apt to believe that it will be celebrated by succeeding generations as the great anniversary festival. It ought to be commemorated as the day of deliverance, by solemn acts of devotion to God Almighty. It ought to be solemnized with pomp and parade, with shows, games, sports, guns, bells, bonfires, and illuminations, from one end of this continent to the other, from this time forward forever more.

—John Adams writing to his wife on July 3, 1776,
the day after the Declaration of Independence
was adopted by the Continental Congress

IT IS NOT SO COMMON FOR NATIONS TO HAVE BIRTHDAYS. What is the birthday of England, for example? When did there begin to be a France or a China or an India? Old and wonderful places, their beginnings are lost in the mists of time. What they are today is connected to their past in ways we can hardly guess.

In the United States we have a birthday, the Fourth of July. This birthday is unusual simply for the fact of its existence, but also for

3

another reason. On the one hand, it is a specific day, marked in memory of specific things done by specific people in a specific place. On the other hand, it is a day for the ages and for everywhere. What these people did, they did in the name of something universal and transcendent. In the combination of these two qualities, our birthday is unprecedented.

The story of our great nation has unfolded under the influence of this combination. Our great controversies and struggles have hinged on our allegiance to it. Our survival has sometimes hung by a thread of attachment to it. It does so right now. Our form of government, I will argue, was established in our Constitution to institute and to guard this combination.

The Declaration of Independence and the Constitution are commanding things for Americans because of this combination of features. On the one hand, they are ours, made by our own fathers. They provided the pattern according to which we have settled a continent and become a great nation, significant to all peoples. Our children, like our fathers and mothers, learn (even if not well) of the Declaration of Independence and the Constitution as they grow up. The way we talk, the way we stand, the way we dance or sing—all are influenced by the laws of our land and the principles behind them, and our laws and principles spring from these two documents.

On the other hand, the document adopted on our birthday speaks with a voice far beyond our fathers and their particular situation, even though that situation was urgent to the point of life and death. Its language is so elevated that its meaning cannot be confined to the situation of its own time and place, to the situation of our own time and place, or to the situation of any time and place. This at least is what it says. If it is wrong about this, then it is wrong about the most important thing.

This universal feature of our birthday reinforces the strength of its calling. If your father gives you an instruction from your upbringing, and then he repeats that instruction in his will, this is powerful. If he himself has risked all that he has to sustain this instruction, and if he has lived his entire life in support of it, this is more powerful. If in addition this instruction claims that it is the right instruction, not just for his life and for yours, but for all lives and for all time, that is most powerful. And yet you cannot base your allegiance to the principle solely on the testimony of your ancestors. You must base your allegiance on the merits of the claim. You must adopt it because it seems sensible, and if it does not, you must discard it—and with it your birthright.

This is the nature of the Declaration of Independence and of the Constitution written pursuant to it. They are our birthright. We Americans owe them a debt. They make a series of demanding claims. Although they leave plenty of room for adaptation to transient things, their core meaning is said to be absolute and fixed. To believe them is to take on the obligation to obey them, and then one must live in a certain way.

One can see how we might come to resent this burden. It is heavy. Its obligations come from more than one source, and therefore they command in more than one way. They command by blood, and they command by principle. They command with the authority of family, and they speak with the awesome force of nature and the God who presides over it. Who would blame us to ask why we should be trapped in this way? Our fathers were revolutionaries. Should we not be the same?

Moreover, we have made so very much progress from the time of the Revolution, from the time of the horse and buggy and the powdered wig. We face new challenges, but also we have all the new tools of modern science. Could we not come up with better principles than our fathers, just as we can now build taller and more momentous structures?[1]

· · · · ·

In relation to our beginning, our history has moved in two modes. Sometimes we have endeavored to embrace—and sometimes we have endeavored to escape—the laws of nature and of nature's God. They have been the source of our liberation, and they have seemed the source of our confining. Sometimes we would enjoy their blessings, but other times we would shrug them off as a curse.

Many of us today reject the universal and timeless claims of the Declaration, and therefore also we reject the forms of government established in the Constitution. We follow the notion, born among academics, that no such claim can be true and no such forms can abide. This belief is very strong among Americans now, and it has made vast achievements in changing our government. Because of this, we are near a moment of choice. This book aims to make clear the terms of that choice. The reader will not be surprised to learn that the author favors the keeping of the birthright, for its beauty and consistency, and for the failings of the alternative. Admitting this sharpens the obligation both of reader and of author to think as clearly, as truthfully, and as fairly as can be. We must do our best.

This book will explore the connection between the Declaration of Independence and the Constitution of the United States. It will state the case for them made by those who wrote and adopted them. It will compare this case to the one made by their contemporary enemies. These are the points that we must consider before we make the choice that is fast upon us.

~ Two ~

DIVIDE AND CONQUER

ON OCTOBER 22, 2009, A REPORTER ASKED SPEAKER OF THE
House Nancy Pelosi, "Where specifically does the Constitution grant
Congress the authority to enact an individual health insurance man-
date?" She replied, "Are you serious? Are you serious?"[1]

Just a few months later, on March 21, 2010, the House of
Representatives passed the Patient Protection and Affordable Care
Act, which establishes that individual mandate in law. An hour before
the vote, Speaker Pelosi spoke "with great pride and great humility."
She said that by passing the act, the House would "honor the vows of
our Founders, who, in the Declaration of Independence, said that we
are endowed by our Creator with certain inalienable rights and among
these are life, liberty, and the pursuit of happiness."[2]

It seems that Speaker Pelosi likes one of the two great pillars of our
Founding, but not the other. The Declaration is a thing to be honored
with pride and humility, but only by means that have no reference to the
Constitution. The two great documents are disconnected in her mind.
They are the two sides of a house divided, straining to pull it apart.

Nor is her reverence for the Declaration quite what it seems. No one who wrote that document defined the term *right* to mean free health care or to justify a law requiring all with money to purchase medical insurance so that those with none may have it for free.[3] Just as the Speaker abandons the Constitution, so she alters the meaning of the Declaration. Nor is she alone. She stands in a long line of statesmen and academics who regard both documents in a very different light from those who wrote them. We Americans have today very mixed views about the meaning and merit of our major Founding documents. We may like the one or the other, but few of us are devoted to them both in the sense in which they are written.

Consider the Declaration. Nearly anyone has to admit that there is something to be said for it. Universal in scope and divine in elevation, it is written in tones of majesty. It celebrates blessings that come directly from God and are known through the reason with which He created us. It proclaims the inclusion of every human being—past, present, and future—in its reach. No nation is left out. No era is excluded. People in the streets of Cairo or Havana, protesting the modern military despots who rule over them, may call upon it for justification. The Hungarians of 1956, crushed by Soviet tanks, uttered its phrases with their last gasps of freedom. The helots under the Spartan lash, the slave-rowers squandering their substance in the Roman galleys, are wrapped in its embracing principles.

On the other hand, there seems to be something implausible and restricting about the Declaration. Its chief author, Thomas Jefferson, might have sided in principle with the helot slaves, but in practice he was a slaveholder like their Spartan masters. And why should he not be a slaveholder, some think, as he was founding a regime that vaunts self-interest and worships in the church of taking care of oneself? That is the trouble with America, according to this view: its people thrive too much at the expense of their neighbors. Is their Founding even good? And who are these Founders, anyway, to lecture us about right and wrong? Who are they to say that there is one truth for every age and time, one set of principles to command us today? We live in an age so modern as to make their quill pens and their bowing absurd. These absolute phrases seemed liberating then but seem constraining today. We have done so much more than those men in their powdered wigs. Why should they tell us the rules under which we must live?

These sentiments go back as far as the time before the Civil War and continue to the present day. The proslavery statesman John Calhoun, offended by its proclamation of equality, called the Declaration "the most false and dangerous of all political errors."[4] Modern thinkers believe it—for all its pretensions of eternal scope—not to transcend but to reflect the time in which it was written. Woodrow Wilson said that it was obsolete, written for an age that believed in the theories of Isaac Newton and regarded government as a mechanism. That age, Wilson believed, was now superseded by Darwin and the theory of evolution, which allows us to see that government is a living organism, one that must change over time.[5] Colonel House, a close advisor to Wilson, wrote a novel in which the hero says, "Our Constitution and our laws served us well for the first hundred years of our existence, but under the condition of today they are not only obsolete, but even grotesque."[6] For John Dewey, the Constitution's view of liberty was "relative to the forces that at a given time and place are increasingly felt to be oppressive."[7] For Frank Goodnow, founder of the American Political Science Association, its claims were the "result of the then existing social conditions."[8]

This means that the perspective of the Founders is worse, in an important respect, than the typical relic of the past. The Spartan masters could justify their tyranny over the helot slaves by the dictates of their own gods, by the authority of their own valor, or by the love of their own families and interests. Their example is therefore less likely to spread, and it makes fewer claims on other places and times. The Declaration of Independence has larger pretensions, and if it is wrong, it is therefore more wrong, and more likely to constrain and interfere with the evolving standards of right that must come later. The idea of the "Laws of Nature and of Nature's God" would then be not a universal but a parochial idea, distinguished only because it is aggressive. It spreads like a virus and resists treatment with the same stubbornness.

· · · · ·

Consider the US Constitution. It, too, must be regarded with a measure of respect. It is the longest surviving written constitution in all of history. For more than two centuries, it has provided a stable and free government for a nation that has increased manyfold in territory and population. It has grown across a continent and welcomed new states and new citizens upon an equal footing with the original. Its dominion has extended across the plains and the mountains to a distant ocean never seen by its Framers. It has welcomed and naturalized immigrants on a scale unknown to any other nation.

It has survived a great Civil War, still our nation's costliest war, during which its larger purpose of freedom was vindicated against the three compromises in its original text with human slavery. It has succeeded when our nation was remote from the great powers. It has succeeded through the great world wars and across a long era in which our power has been felt in every corner of the globe.

It has succeeded in an agrarian society. It has succeeded through the Industrial Revolution, through the jet age, and into the information age. It has survived, impaired but intact, through more than a century of organized opposition to its procedures and limits. Still today it commands the hearts of most Americans, and still today it places inconveniences in the way of those who would overcome it. In the making of fundamental law, there has been nothing like it. To ascribe its achievements to accident would be a failure of sense and of inquisitiveness.

Yet there seems to be something very annoying about the Constitution. It reads too much like a law, and this is made worse by the fact that it *is* a law. It is full of things you have to do and other things you may not do. It relates these things without the poetry of the Declaration. The language of "the Laws of Nature and of Nature's God" stirs the heart and persists in the memory. The constitutional language requiring that the yeas and nays be recorded in the House of Representatives is not put so nobly, and that is because it is not so noble a thing. If it were only a detail, perhaps we could abide it better. Alas, the details in the Constitution are not only details, but also rules, rules that are especially awkward to change. They feel an awful lot like fetters.

Its being so bossy and its not being so inspiring, the Constitution has often been the object of controversy. The convention that drafted it was fractious for months. The debates through which it was ratified took years to reach agreement. Its fundamental arrangements were contested in the Civil War. All of this was before modern times, when the opposition has become serious.

Our modern elites in the academy, in journalism, and in politics regard the Constitution as a relic. They say every kind of negative against its meaning, its goodness, its relevance, its scope, its legality, its advisability, its comprehensibility, its connection or harmony with the rest of the Founding and especially with the Declaration of Independence. This practice has now persisted so long as to become tradition, nearly half as old as the Constitution itself.

In the end the modern opposition to the Declaration and the Constitution stems from the same source. The Founders understood the documents to be connected, to supply together the principles and the details of government, to be a persuasive and durable unity. The early leaders of the Progressive movement—Wilson, Dewey, Goodnow, and their friends—were opponents of them both. This proved a poor strategy politically. The words of the Declaration have a way of continuing to ring across the ages. The arrangements of the Constitution have a way of organizing our actions so as to produce certain results, and they have done this more reliably than any governing instrument in the history of man. Connect these arrangements to the beauty of the Declaration, and one has something inspiring *and* commanding. The Declaration acquires a practical form and operation that do not seem to come from it alone. The Constitution soars to the elevation of the natural law, and its arrangements are reinforced with that strength.

Franklin Roosevelt, one of the most important of our presidents, found a way to overcome the obstacle presented by the combination of our Founding documents. He divorced them. He embraced the Declaration, and thereby he brought liberalism back to the vocabulary, if not to the meaning, of the American Founding. To Roosevelt, the Declaration of Independence contains, sure enough, eternal truths, and the business of government is, sure enough, to protect rights. But, continues Roosevelt, "the task of statesmanship has always been the redefinition of these rights in terms of the changing and growing social order."[9] Rights are eternal, but we define them anew in each generation. And if rights change, the steps required for their protection change too. In the result, the Declaration of Independence retains its place of honor and authority (however altered our understanding of it), but the Constitution is demoted. Its structure is too inflexible to accommodate the changing needs of government and the people it will manage. Either it must go, or its structure must be regarded as elastic.

. . . . .

The innovations of Dewey, Goodnow, and Wilson, amended by Franklin Roosevelt, are now the established order in the academy and much of politics. One can measure this in the reaction to the opening of Congress in January 2011. The Republicans had won a majority in the House of Representatives. They were benefited by the influence of a movement harkening back even in its name to the American Revolution: the Tea Party. This recalling of the American Revolution extended right down to the opening of a debate all across the land about the meaning of the Constitution. This was no happy development to people like Speaker Pelosi, who think the question of the constitutionality of the health care law not to be a serious question.

The new majority was elected by many who wished it to be a serious question. They noticed that service in the Congress requires that one take an oath to uphold the Constitution. They noticed that the president, all the judges, every senior federal official, and for that matter every member of the United States military are required to take such an oath. They thought, *Why do we not begin the session by reading the Constitution aloud? This will remind us of the object of our oath.*

It was a commonsense idea. But to many, it was infuriating.

To columnist and public intellectual Michael Lind, the Tea Party is an extension of the Confederacy:

> Now that the Republican Party, founded as a northern party opposed to the extension of slavery, is disproportionately a party of white Southern reactionaries, dominated by the political heirs of the Confederates and the segregationist Dixiecrats, the denunciation of many exercises of federal authority as illegitimate would have been predictable, even if the president were not a black Yankee from Abraham Lincoln's Illinois.[10]

To columnist E. J. Dionne, the Tea Party and the Republicans are going to stimulate much-needed debate, and in that debate they will be proved wrong. He quotes scholar Gordon Wood: we "can recognize the extraordinary character of the Founding Fathers while also knowing that those 18th-century political leaders were not outside history. . . . They were as enmeshed in historical circumstances as we are, they had no special divine insight into politics."[11]

This is on the surface a mild criticism, but would be devastating to our Constitution if true. The central claim of the Founders is that they were acting on principles that transcend time and place. They committed treason in the name of those principles. They killed and were killed for them. To say that they were simply creatures of their time is to take from them the rock upon which they built, to deprive them of the reason upon which they based all. Moreover, Dionne and Wood expose themselves to a certain objection. If everyone is trapped by his time and place in history, what about *them*? What about Dionne and Wood? How do they know that their statements about the Founders are valid unless they are able to stand "outside history"? How do they know, as an objective proposition, that the Founders were trapped inside their time?

A superior example of this line of thought is provided by a 2010 Constitution Day speech given by Harvard law professor Michael Klarman.[12] He gave the speech to help Johns Hopkins University achieve its mandatory annual commemoration of the Constitution, which is required by federal law of all colleges and universities that receive federal aid. In the US Code, this requirement comes under the rubric of "Patriotic Observances."[13] If by *patriotic* we mean love and loyalty for the things of our fathers, most such occasions do not much serve the purpose. But universities hold the celebrations anyway, as large sums are at stake. Neither this kind of regulation nor the money that comes with it has any precedent before the late 1950s in the United States, and so their constitutionality is controversial. Indeed Professor Klarman believes them unconstitutional, and he says so in this very speech. He thinks the regulations should continue anyway. This makes a nice irony at the foundation of these celebrations. The irony deepens the more one observes.

Professor Klarman's Constitution Day speech is an extended condemnation of "constitutional idolatry." By that, he does not mean worshiping the Constitution as a god, but respecting it as a good. Under four headings, he argues that it is not good:

1. The Constitution represents "values" we should abhor. Here he refers especially to the three places in which the Constitution protects the institution of slavery. He has a point here, even if he destroys the ground upon which the point can

stand. We shall have a lot to say about the practice of slavery among the Founders later.

2. It imposes upon us practices that we "would never freely choose" and that are "impossible to defend based on contemporary values." Here he means the features of the Constitution that are not purely democratic or that do not assign the same weight to each vote, such as the Electoral College, two senators per state without regard to state population, and (for some reason) the requirement that one be a native-born citizen to serve as president.

3. It is "irrelevant to the current political design of our nation." Here in a most telling point he describes the modern administrative state, which he says flatly is unconstitutional and yet superior.

4. It does not protect our rights very much and not as well as our own "political and social mores."

Following Franklin Roosevelt, Professor Klarman denounces the Constitution in the name of the rights it was formed to protect. He does this in the name of the people, arguing that they deserve a government that is closer to them and that provides each individual an equal voice. The "Framers," he says, "were trying to create a powerful national government that was as distant from popular control as possible."

The heart of the matter is in point three, concerning the new administrative state with which the Constitution is incompatible. According to Klarman, the administrative state is at once a "vitally important fourth branch" and "almost certainly unconstitutional in multiple ways according to the original design of the Framers." He does not say in so many words that he likes this new fourth branch, but clearly he does. Otherwise, he would complain of its existence rather than criticize the Constitution for not authorizing it. If bigamy is illegal, but everyone has two wives, you might complain about the law, or you might complain about the two wives. Which you choose is revealing.

Where, one wonders, is the legitimacy for this fourth branch? Professor Klarman mentions that the courts have upheld it. But the courts get their authority from the Constitution, and each judge is required in the Constitution to swear to uphold the Constitution. The Constitution gets its authority, in turn, from ratifying conventions held in each state to which delegates were popularly elected. If a judge defies the Constitution, then he breaks his oath, and he overcomes an expression of the popular will. In that case, the acts of judges become rather like the Senate that Professor Klarman criticizes: they are not responsive to the will of the people, at least as that will is measured by legal acts taken by the people.

The same points apply to the other two branches. Congress created the administrative agencies by laws. Congress gets its authority from the Constitution, and its members swear to uphold the Constitution. The president signed these laws creating these agencies (except in the cases where his veto was overridden). The president gets his authority from the same place, and takes the same oath, as the members of Congress. Why then is it a good thing that the Constitution is violated by people who are sworn to uphold it?

The answer seems to be that this fourth branch conforms to our "political and social mores," which Professor Klarman identifies as the surest protection of our rights. The trouble with this is that these political and social mores do not always prevail. They did not prevail in the Confederacy, for example. There slave owners whipped their slaves if they ran away and worked many of them to death if they did not. Political and social mores vary widely about the world even today, and in many places the trend is not good for the mores that Professor Klarman favors. Is there security in this standard? In the excellent play *A Man for All Seasons*, which chronicles Thomas More's last years, More says to his impetuous son-in-law that the wind would blow very hard if all the laws were cut down.[14] The same might be said for the Constitution.

What, one wonders, does Professor Klarman like about the character of this new fourth branch? After all, he complains that government under the Constitution is not directly or equally representative in the cases of the Senate and the Electoral College. Yet these new administrative agencies are infamously unrepresentative, and notoriously they break the society down into parts and treat different parts of it differently. Those that regulate business are often captured by and favor the particular firms that lead their industries. Those that regulate people have their favorites: some ethnic groups get protected, some do not; some regions get protected, some do not; women, in the majority, are grouped with minorities for protection and therefore form part of a large majority—but we call it a minority anyway.

Moreover, the powers of these agencies are both sweeping and sealed off from accountability to the people. Many agencies combine all three powers of government in the hands of their senior administrators. They make the regulations, which have the force of law. They enforce them on companies and individuals, states and local governments. They fine and bring charges that can lead to imprisonment. And then, when the poor souls who are burdened, fined, and accused wish to appeal, they go before the agency into whose clutches they have already fallen. For years, the South Coast Air Quality Management District in Southern California had about 10 percent of its staff doing public relations. It built a wonderful complex atop a hill in Southern California for its accommodation. Its staff grew to a vast size. All this was funded from fees and fines that it levied on the groups that it regulated, and so naturally they became cowed, afraid to say anything bad about the agency in the newspaper.

In his speech Professor Klarman remarks with pride that a man may call the president a socialist without fear of punishment. Use that latitude, if you dare, before a regulator and see what you get. Or consider the attitude toward freedom of speech by the regulatory "czar," if you can believe we have such an official in the United States, one Cass Sunstein (another law professor), who holds that the government should allocate the right to speak to make sure everyone gets a fair chance.[15]

The Consumer Financial Protection Bureau, launched in July 2011, was designed by a colleague of Professor Klarman on the Harvard faculty. Its budget does not come from congressional appropriation; therefore there is no ability in principle for elected branches to tailor its cost to overall public priorities. Instead it gets its funds from a percentage of the revenues of the Federal Reserve, which are themselves locked in a dark box that Congress has been trying to crack open for years.

Such agencies exemplify the administrative state. As that state was conceived in elitism, so now it proceeds in privilege and mere credentialing. The classes of its elevated minions are now tenured and expensive—and still they feel martyred. The whole system is arbitrary, complex, and shrouded in mystery. To plead before it requires lawyers and lobbyists who command vast salaries, and so they are available not to the ordinary but to the well heeled and entrenched. Or else they are provided at subsidized rates to selected constituencies, who then become wards or partial wards of those who manage the subsidies. Taxpayers foot the bill and are blamed for their selfishness at the same time.

Why should a man such as Professor Klarman favor such a thing? He is a man of liberal sentiment. He acts without doubt from good motives and possesses enormous gifts of intellect and character. Why would he favor the modern bureaucracy over the Constitution of the United States? Why should he regard the Constitution as odious in principle, an albatross when it is effective, and for the most part happily irrelevant? Thinking these things, why should he make the Constitution his chosen field of study?

The answer has to do with a change in our understanding of rights and what it takes to protect them. These regulatory agencies are designed to accommodate an evolutionary standard of rights favored in the academic world for generations now. In this understanding, the Constitution is severed from the Declaration, and both are compromised. The Declaration proclaims rights that are inadequate, and the standards by which it proclaims them are obsolete. This being so, the Constitution is simply destroyed. Its arrangements are outmoded and rightly ignored. Its purposes are rejected, and we are left with nothing except the tide of history (characterized by supporters of the administrative state as "progress") to guide us. In modern America this tide has all the force of bureaucracy behind it.

Before we give in to that tide completely, it is worth asking, Did the Declaration of Independence and the Constitution of the United States ever have much to do with each other? Do they partake of the strength of each other? Are they in fact intended to be what Abraham Lincoln called them, an apple of gold in a frame of silver?[16] Are they made of precious metal or of dross?

⌐ THREE ⌐

DIVORCE: THE DECLARATION AND THE CONSTITUTION ESTRANGED?

EVEN AMONG HISTORIANS WHO ADMIRE BOTH THE Declaration and the Constitution, the divorce between them has long since been accepted as fact. Popular historian Joseph Ellis, who has done good writing about the Founding, presents a moderate and balanced version of it:

> A corollary triumph [of the Revolutionary generation] that merits mention is the ability to reconcile two competing and, in several respects, contradictory political impulses. There were really two founding moments: the first in 1776, which declared American independence, and the second in 1787–88, which declared American nationhood. The Declaration of Independence is the seminal document in the first instance, the Constitution in the second. The former is a radical document that locates sovereignty in the individual and depicts government as an alien force, making rebellion

against it a natural act. The latter is a conservative document that locates sovereignty in that collective called "the people," makes government an essential protector of liberty rather than its enemy, and values social balance over personal liberation. It is extremely rare for the same political elite to straddle both occasions. Or, to put it differently, it is uncommon for the same men who make a revolution also to secure it.[1]

Now, this is a handsome passage, and one cannot help but admire Professor Ellis's friendliness toward the Declaration, the Constitution, and the Founders who wrote them.

To Professor Ellis, the Constitution is conservative, and the Declaration is liberal. To him, the Declaration and the Constitution are nearly, if not fully, incompatible.[2] They are oil and water, and he likes them both, just as anyone may like both oil and water. But they are very different things.

There is something to this on the surface. Obviously the purpose of the Declaration is different from that of the Constitution. One throws off a government; the other builds one. One liberates; the other regulates. One defies rules; the other imposes them. One is bold and universal; the other is specific and restrained. One was written mainly by Jefferson, airy of manner as he was elevated of height. The other was written mainly by Madison, logical and precise, his reasoning as compact as his tiny figure. Like its author, the Declaration shows imagination and eloquence. Like its author, the Constitution shows order and balance.

But are they really so different? There is the problem that their authors did not think so. It happens that Jefferson and Madison were the deepest of friends, both personal and political, for nearly all of their adult lives. They cooperated closely in building the nation, including the political party that would govern it for two generations and elect each of them president, one after the other. They had differences, true enough, but no two men of such stature ever made a better or more enduring partnership or shared so many purposes and principles high and commanding.

If the men were reconciled so profoundly, it is likely the documents they produced were also reconciled. Read the Declaration for a minute, and one sees certain problems with the way Professor Ellis characterizes it. The professor writes, for example, that the Declaration "depicts government as an alien force." Where does it do that?

The opening of the Declaration speaks of peoples. The first right it names is the right not of an individual, but of a people. It is peoples, not individuals, who are entitled under the "Laws of Nature and of Nature's God" to a "separate and equal station." This must mean that peoples have a standing in nature—that it is natural for people to form peoples. If that is natural, then government is not an alien but a natural force. And that term *natural* comes from an ancient word for "birth." Government is therefore not an alien, but natural born.

Professor Ellis writes that the Declaration makes "rebellion against [government] a natural act." True enough: it says, "Whenever any Form of Government becomes destructive to these ends [namely, securing the rights of each and every man], it is the Right of the People to alter or to abolish it." Notice it says that this is a right of "the People," the group entitled in nature to a certain standing. This group may indeed throw off the government if it pleases. What then is it to do? Jefferson continues that the next step is to "institute new Government." The institution of new government is parallel in grammar, in meaning, and in priority to the right to throw off government. If it is natural for a people to rebel against a bad government, it is also natural for a people to establish a new one that is good.

This is reiterated as the Declaration proceeds. The document has much to say about the form and nature of government, especially in its long middle section, which is generally ignored today. It was not ignored at the time, however, because this section contains the charges against the king and Parliament that give specific justification for the act of revolution. This part puts the responsibility directly on the British government. It builds a case against that government, specifically, in one of the monumental controversies in all history. At stake is the loyalty of a whole people to the king. And at stake is the vast land upon which they live, at that time still unknown in extent, but the prize possession of one of the greatest empires in the entire human story. America is the chief British holding in what is called "the New World," a place of such proportion and gravity as to constitute a whole other sphere.

The charges against the king name the specific practical ground upon which all this is to be taken from him. It is little wonder that the king and his ministers would take pains to answer the Declaration. They do so in part by a legal brief that we will describe later.[3] That legal brief, it is no surprise, focuses on this middle section.

Now, the Revolution is justified in the first instance and in general by the laws of nature and of nature's God, and the self-evident truth of human equality, which are named in the opening sentences of the Declaration. But these are not by themselves enough. The Declaration says that "Governments long established should not be changed for light and transient causes." It is only "when a long train of abuses and usurpations . . . evinces a design to reduce them under absolute Despotism" that it becomes both the right and the "duty" of the people to "throw off such Government."

This means that in these charges against the king and Parliament, everything is at stake. The Declaration in this respect is a syllogism.[4] The major premise is that governments are formed (and necessary) to protect our natural rights. The minor premises are to be found in these claims of despotism against the British. The conclusion is that the American people are justified to declare their independence, and they do so. If the premises are true, then the conclusion follows necessarily.

This means that the Declaration supplies both an example and a principle. The principle is stated beautifully in its opening sentences. It is universal in its scope and application. Each individual is born with unalienable rights. Individuals come together to form peoples, and each people has a natural standing to a separate and equal station.

No man may be governed except by his consent. No people may be governed except by its consent.

The Declaration also gives examples to indicate how government should be organized. The rights of the individual and the duties of government are reciprocal: if an individual has a right, then the government has a duty to protect it. If the government does not, then the individual is justified in joining with others to throw off the government.

.   .   .   .   .

The list of charges against the king has a curious feature. It is not just a list of the individual rights that the king has violated. There are several of them, and they are important. In addition, there are several things the king has done that concern no direct action on individuals ("depriving us . . . of the benefits of Trial by Jury"), but rather the manner in which the government is arranged ("dissolved Representative Houses"; "made Judges dependent on his Will alone"). Both the infringements of individual rights and the misarrangements of government are stated emphatically and with little qualification. The evil of them is apparent on their face; the fact that they have happened is, by itself, the cause of revolution. For this reason, they provide guidance almost as comprehensive in their application as the universal principles named at the beginning of the Declaration. Whenever these things happen, the people are justified in throwing off their government. Any government that commits these evils forfeits its legitimacy. Such a government has no claim upon the loyalty of its people.

The Declaration does say that whenever the people throw off a government and institute a new one, they may lay "its foundation on such principles" and organize "its powers in such form, as to them shall seem most likely to effect their Safety and Happiness." No one may prescribe precisely or in complete detail the forms under which a people may organize its government. On the other hand, any government must derive its "just powers from the consent of the governed" if its powers are to be justly derived. A people who granted to its rulers absolute authority to rule over it would be a foolish and wrong-headed people, destined for misery. The Declaration provides guidance on this point and others.

This guidance includes several matters of form that must be present in government for it to be trustworthy and effective in its function. The violations of these key features of government are among the particular cause of the Revolution. One might say, in short, that every government must be so *constituted* as to prevent these evils. In this fact is to be found the *constitutional* view of the Declaration of Independence. The Declaration uses the term *constitution* once only, and it uses it in the singular. It refers to the apparently existing constitution of the Americans: "He has combined with others to subject us to a jurisdiction foreign to our *constitution*, and unacknowledged by our laws; giving his Assent to their Acts of pretended Legislation" (emphasis added).

This constitution that exists among the Americans is not, it seems, a written constitution. Whatever it is, it is only one thing. One may surmise from the rest of the text in this section of the Declaration that it includes some authority for the king and Parliament in Great Britain, but also it includes the whole system of colonial government, the representative bodies, the courts, the town meetings. These arrangements are different from those of the foreign jurisdiction to which the king is wrongfully subjecting the people of America. They are different because they operate with the consent of the governed.

Begin at the beginning of this list of complaints. The first of them is, of course, the most prominent: who can miss the first thing in a list? The answer is, many people can miss it, including many of high intellectual accomplishment. Apparently Professor Ellis missed it when he says that in the Declaration, government is regarded as an "alien force." On the contrary, the first complaint of the Declaration says of the king: "He has refused his Assent to Laws, the most wholesome and necessary for the public good."

"Wholesome and necessary" are not synonyms for "alien." In the Declaration laws and government are not alien. To the contrary, when they are wholesome, they are "necessary for the public good." Apparently to be without such laws is to live in anarchy or despotism, which are unnatural and miserable states. Governments have the duty to provide these laws. A monarch who fails to provide them forfeits his claim to rule. The American Revolution is not justified by the fact that government is an alien force. The truth is the opposite: the Revolution is justified by the fact that government is necessary. The king has sometimes failed to provide it, and other times he has provided it in ways that subvert the purpose of government.

Not only the first, but also the second and the third charges against the king concern the necessity of government. The king has forbidden his governors to pass laws except after long delays to wait for the king to make up his mind about them. Also he has refused to agree to laws that the people need for their well-being, unless the colonies should first agree to give up the right of representation. The right of representation, we shall see, is fundamental to the American Founding. Here the Declaration says that the right of representation is "inestimable" to the people and "formidable to tyrants only."

Some laws are apparently wholesome, and some laws are not. The justification for revolution consists in this distinction between good laws and bad. This distinction—and by extension the distinction between just and unjust government—is the fundamental concern of political science from its birth in the classical world. It seems to be a fundamental concern of the Founders too. When the Declaration demands laws "wholesome and necessary for the public good," it raises the question what kinds of laws those are. The rest of the charges against the British provide an outline of these laws and their chief characteristics.

There are seventeen paragraphs in this middle section of the Declaration. They take up 652 of the document's 1,320 words, or just under half. They may be understood in three categories, and these three categories are congruent with those that form the structure of the Constitution and its rationale, as especially James Madison explains that rationale in the *Federalist*.

. . . . .

The first category is representation. James Madison writes that the Constitution is distinguished from all its predecessors in being a purely representative form of government. No government either ancient or modern had accomplished the "total exclusion of the people" from a share in the actual operation of the government.[5] As we shall see in chapter 8, Madison regarded this distinction as pivotal. It makes possible decisive advantages, especially two: the location of sovereignty outside the government and the separation of powers. The structure of the Constitution and its specific genius are found in these two features. Both features are forecast in the Declaration, and this is no accident. The rallying cry of the American Revolution, after all, had been "no taxation without representation."

The right and principle of representation is proclaimed in numbers three through six of the Declaration's charges against the British, right after and intermingled with the charge that the king has failed to provide government. The third of the complaints states that he has "refused to pass other Laws for the accommodation of large districts of people, unless those people would relinquish the right of Representation in the Legislature, a right inestimable to them and formidable to tyrants only." The right of representation has therefore a value beyond any estimating. Notice how, in this passage, the king has placed one right in conflict with another: if the people want laws, they must agree that he alone gets to make them, giving up their right to be represented. That is the practice of what the Declaration calls "a tyrant."

The Declaration recites several specific ways in which the right of representation has been obstructed. The king has called legislatures together "at places unusual, uncomfortable, and distant from the depository of their public Records." He has dissolved them repeatedly.

After their dissolution he has refused the election of replacements. Nonetheless, no king can deprive the people of their ultimate powers of legislation. Those powers are "incapable of Annihilation," and so they have "returned to the People at large for their exercise."

This implies that the vehicle of representation is a proxy for the direct making of laws by the sovereign people. When representation is obstructed, the laws revert to the control of the rightful sovereign— the people who are to live under them. The Declaration does not say anything in criticism of this direct form of democracy, although later many of the Founders would do so.[6] The consensus of the Founding generation is that representative institutions are an essential feature of government that is both stable and free and the only kind adaptable to the New World.[7] For its part, the Declaration fiercely defends representative institutions.

To make a government purely representative alters the operation and the effect of government in far-reaching ways. This begins with the simple fact that representation requires two parties. There must be someone who is represented, and there must be someone who represents. In this way representative government makes the people distinct from the government. This has larger effects than one might guess.

For one thing, to appoint a representative is an alternative to doing it oneself. Neville Chamberlain's brother Austen once wrote to Winston Churchill (with whom he was friendly) that he had declined to discuss certain business with foreign statesmen because that business was Churchill's responsibility. He referred them to Churchill with the words: ". . . it is unnecessary to bark oneself when one keeps a dog."[8] Likewise, if you keep a representative, you let him make the laws.

Now, obviously the dog and the representative are the subjects of their masters. A wild dog need obey nothing except his natural instincts; a domesticated dog must obey the will of his master. Similarly an absolute king holds his authority in his own person and must obey only his own will. A representative, on the other hand, is accountable to the people on behalf of whom he rules. He is not his own master.

His status as a representative is a limited status. (It is also a station of great dignity and therefore not doglike.) To be the representative of a free people is to be an elevated thing indeed. It is so elevated that the Founders thought it the highest station to which they could aspire. It is not, however, to hold an absolute power or to hold any power in one's own right.

Having said this, one must also realize that it is not only the representative who is limited by the purely representative arrangements of the American Revolution. Think about the man who keeps a dog and is relieved of the necessity of barking. He also gives up some of the opportunity to bark (it is hard to be heard over a barking dog). Likewise, if you keep a representative, you deprive yourself of the ability to make laws directly. You must wait for an election. You may throw the representative out, but only when it is time to vote. If in the meantime you become angry with the representative, you may write him a letter or say dirty things about him in the newspaper. Indeed it is an advantage that you may do these things because you are compelled to think and talk rather than to act. James Madison had a particular belief in the power of public discourse to make the nation and the public better.[9] This follows from a belief that thinking before acting is a hallmark of human excellence. Therefore it is an advantage that the sovereign people of our country have plenty of time to talk and many fewer opportunities to act. That is a good situation in which to place anyone who holds the final authority. And while the people talk, their representatives will still hold their offices until the next time there is a vote. And they will be cast out only if a sufficient number of the citizens want that to happen.

In other words, representation provides a restraint upon the ruled as well as upon the rulers. In this sense, too, it is an institution of limited government.

· · · · ·

The second category into which the charges against the king are arranged is limited government. One can see how limited government would be necessary for there to be a form of government that is purely representative. Government is a very powerful thing. It is natural to people: they always form governments and make laws. Wherever there are laws, the laws have a monopoly on force. To place control of that force in a people who are entirely outside the government is to forbid ultimate control of that force to the people who are *in* government. For the people *outside* government to be strong enough to hold that force in check requires that there be a large and vibrant private society—a society full of families, churches, businesses, charities, clubs, and teams. All of these operate independently of the government and are able to ask, to paraphrase some famous words, not what their government can do for them, but what they can do for their government. If the government is too large in relation to the private sphere, it will dominate. A government that is *not* too large is the old meaning of the term *liberal government*. It has come to mean something rather different today. But more on that later.

In any case, there can be no doubt that the men who wrote the Declaration, and the generation who rallied to its cry, favored this liberal kind of society in the old sense. After all, they had come across the great ocean and made their way in a wilderness. They had built their governments by their own contrivance and with almost no help from the people back home, especially the monarch. They were used to doing for themselves, and they thought they ought to continue to do it. It was not just that they valued their freedom, although they valued that very much. They were accustomed to being rulers, to exercising self-government over themselves and in concert with their fellow citizens over the whole nation, and this was precious to them. They felt that they were made for it.

Some of the strongest words in the Declaration of Independence concern this matter of limited government. One can see from the chain of events that led to the Declaration how the colonists feared that they were losing control of their lives. They had achieved so much and learned so much about the art of government while achieving it. And then emissaries from the king, including armed forces, began to appear to enforce the will of London. The Declaration declared in response:

> He has erected a multitude of New Offices, and sent hither swarms of Officers to harrass our people, and eat out their substance.
> He has kept among us, in times of peace, Standing Armies without the Consent of our legislatures.
> He has affected to render the Military independent of and superior to the Civil power.
> He has combined with others to subject us to a jurisdiction foreign to our constitution, and unacknowledged by our laws; giving his Assent to their Acts of pretended Legislation:
>
> > For Quartering large bodies of armed troops among us:
> > For protecting them, by mock Trial, from punishment for any Murders which they should commit on the Inhabitants of these States:
> > For cutting off our Trade with all parts of the world:
> > For imposing Taxes on us without our Consent.

This is the source of the wrath of the American people in the Founding generation. They had built a society of self-government. They would live in no other kind. Representation depends on this kind of society and also makes it possible. There can be no doubt that the Declaration proposes a government of limited scope; it is a fighting document, written to defend that kind of government to the death.

· · · · ·

The third category of charges against the king concerns the separation of powers, which forms the organizing principle of the Constitution and is fundamental to its operation. It is fundamental to the Declaration too.

Separation of powers is an arrangement by which the main functions of government are divided into different hands. These "functions" of government are simply the three main things a government must do in order to operate. First, it must make the laws, the rules by which people live together. This is the legislative function. Second, the laws have to be "executed," meaning that the army must be organized and commanded; taxes, alas, must be collected and spent for the purposes prescribed in the law; lawbreakers must be caught and restrained. This is the executive function. Third, cases of dispute that arise under the law must be tried. These cases of dispute arise between private parties: you promised to give me this if I gave you that, and you did not do your part. These are civil cases. Sometimes they arise between the public and a private party: you harmed another person, stole his goods, burned his house, or disturbed the public peace. These are called criminal cases. The function of deciding these cases is the judicial function.

Separation of powers means simply the division of these powers so that no one person or small group may do them all. You can see why this might be important. For one thing, you can see why the king might not like it. In early British political history, which is much longer than the American, kings enjoyed heavy influence in all three areas. If you ran afoul of the king, he could threaten you in a lot of ways. He never had full control of the legislature, but he had plenty of influence, and he could use it to get a law passed that would forbid you to do something that he knew was important to you. In this case he was legislating. The next thing you knew, his bailiffs or marshals or soldiers would come knocking at your door to take you into custody. Then he was executing. Then you would be taken before judges beholden to him, and they would pass down a harsh sentence. Effectively the king was judging.

Over the course of history, the legislative and judicial functions were taken away from the king, and then finally the executive authority, too, and it was placed in the hands of officers accountable to the people. Much blood was spilled along the way. Also along the way political philosophers, especially Montesquieu, made much of this practice of separation of powers that was growing in Great Britain.

Interestingly, the birth of the British Empire and its colonies became the scene of another great controversy over separation of powers. What the king had done to the British people, now the king and Parliament together were attempting to do to the American people.

Separation of powers can be much more firmly maintained in a purely representative system. A system is called "purely" representative because the sovereign has no place in the operation of the government. By "sovereign," we mean the one holding, in any nation, the authority to rule, blessed by the principles held by that nation to be highest and most commanding. In many nations the idea has been that God or the gods appoint certain people to rule. In other nations the idea has been that a certain family was chosen to rule, either because there was something special about that family or because things would not run properly unless some family was chosen, and the rule of this one or that one became hallowed by time. In the American nation government is believed for the first time to serve the high purpose of defending the equal rights of every citizen, that no human being may be rightly governed except by his consent. This doctrine places the people, or rather a majority of them, in control of the government. They are sovereign. All or nearly all of the people believe them to be the ultimate authority, and no one may rightly supersede their will.

In any nation, whoever is the sovereign commands vast authority. The sovereign has the kind of prestige and legitimacy that tends to give it the final say. If the sovereign is in the government, even as only one branch of the government, that branch tends to be the most powerful and to overcome the other branches. In a monarchy, where everyone believes that the king has legitimate title to rule, the monarch often constitutes the executive branch. The legislature and the judiciary tend to give way to him, and there is always the danger that they will lose their separate identity and authority. The history of monarchies is full of such events.

The Founders believed that the same rules applied in a popular government, a government in which authority is vested in the people or in the majority of them. They looked at the democracies of the past, such as Athens in ancient Greece, and they saw a record of turbulence, of inconsistent policy, of impulses and fashions carrying the assembly to the point that harm was done. There are plenty of stories in the ancient histories of the popular assembly of Athens getting angry with a neighbor or colony, dispatching a military force, and soon after reconsidering and sending another force to stop the first. Sometimes both sets of generals were prosecuted, one for suggesting the attack and the other for suggesting retreat.[10]

When the people are sovereign, they are the strongest force, and nothing can stand up to them. Anything in the way of separation of powers tends to collapse. The executive and the judiciary bow before the superior strength of the sovereign majority, and the next thing you know some minority is being oppressed.

In the colonies, and later most famously in the Constitution of the United States, separation of powers is taken to a high state of perfection. And in the Constitution, separation of powers is strengthened by the fact that the government is purely representative. The people, there can be no doubt, are sovereign, but they do not occupy any place in the government. Therefore they can only delegate their powers in pieces: some of the powers to one branch, some of the powers to another branch, some of the powers to local government, and some of the powers to the state and federal governments. There is great safety in delegating the strength of government force in this way.

The Declaration of Independence has several provisions critical of the king for violating this separation of powers. Also a grand theme, the grandest of themes, runs right through the fabric of the

Declaration to emphasize the high authority of the principles that justify the Revolution and the importance of the separation of powers.

The first three of the complaints against the king, the ones concerning his failure to provide government, are also complaints about the violation of the separation of powers. The king and his colonial governors—the executive branch of the colonies—are interfering with the operation of the legislature. They have crossed over a line. The same can be said of the next group of complaints, the ones that concern the king's obstructions of representative government. These, too, are intrusions on the legislative function by the executive.

The Declaration also complains that the king has interfered with the judicial function. He has "obstructed the Administration of Justice, by refusing his Assent to Laws for establishing Judiciary powers." He has "made Judges dependent on his Will alone, for the tenure of their offices, and the amount and payment of their salaries." He has held "mock" trials for his soldiers accused of murder of civilians. An independent judiciary is crucial because it is in the judicial power that the government and the individual meet. If the judges are independent—if they are not dependent on the other branches for their offices or pay, and if they are appointed by a different process than the other branches—then they may look at the case with different eyes than the executive and the legislature. One can see why the king would find this inconvenient. One can see why the colonies would insist that it be maintained.

There is also in the Declaration the grandest indication of the importance of the separation of powers.[11] God is mentioned four times. He appears first in the expression "the Laws of Nature and of Nature's God." He appears next as "Creator." He appears the third time as "the Supreme Judge of the world." And finally, the authors of the Declaration express a "firm reliance on the protection of divine Providence."

God appears, therefore, as each branch of government—legislator, executor, and judge—and as something like a Founder. And the attitude toward God in the Declaration is as the source of perfection, or rather perfection itself. In the great controversy with the mother country, God can be trusted to judge the "rectitude of our intentions." No man can be so trusted. Facing war and death, we can trust "divine Providence" to protect us. Our own powers are apparently insufficient. And the "Laws of Nature and of Nature's God" apply always and must always be obeyed. These are the only laws so applying and so commanding.

· · · · ·

Implicit in this is a fact to which we will return, namely, that the Declaration is as much an act of obedience as it is of rebellion. For now it is safe to conclude that the Declaration supports without variance and profoundly the institution of separation of powers, which gives the Constitution its structure. On the highest level, the Constitution is a simple document. True, it is full of details about how this branch and that branch must operate, and about how this officer or that officer must be appointed or elected. But above that, it reduces simply to the principle of representation, which demands in turn that the government be limited in size and scope in relation to the private society, and which makes possible a firmer system of separation of powers.

Also, there can be no doubt that the Declaration of Independence is built around these same three conceptions. The king is to be discarded because he refuses to act as the representative of the people. In one of the most beautiful passages written during the long controversy that led to the Declaration of Independence, Thomas Jefferson appeals to the king in his *Summary View of the Rights of British America*:

> Open your breast Sire, to liberal and expanded thought. Let not the name of George the Third be a blot in the page of history. You are surrounded by British counsellors, but remember that they are parties. You have no ministers for American affairs, because you have none taken from among us, nor amenable to the laws on which they are to give you advice.[12]

The king is also to be discarded because he has invaded not only the private rights of the individual colonists, regarded in the Declaration as sacred, but also the private realm of a liberal society that must thrive and grow in order to control and benefit from the necessary force given the government.

And finally the king is to be discarded because he has violated the separation of powers, the only device by which a free government can be strong enough to do the necessary job of government and still remain safe, the protector rather than the usurper of the rights of the people.

In this way, the Declaration of Independence argues that the king has styled himself to be like God. But he is not God. And in the firmest possible way, the Founders assert that they will obey God over him or any man.

We may conclude then that the Declaration of Independence does not treat government as an alien force. It says the contrary both positively and negatively. It insists that government be provided to a people, that it be based upon their consent, and that it be arranged so that it can be relied upon to respond to their will and protect their rights. Government being necessary, it matters very much how it is arranged. The Declaration lays the general rules for that arrangement. Those rules, says the Declaration, are to be found in the "Laws of Nature and of Nature's God."

~∽ Four ∾~

The Laws of Nature
and of Nature's God

THE DECLARATION OF INDEPENDENCE WAS BORN, OR RATHER exploded, into an aristocratic world. Sir Thomas More is an example of life at its best and its worst in this world. He rose and fell through the aristocracy. His was a world of nobles, and especially it was a world of kings. The kings were the sons of kings. Their friends and familiars were the dukes and earls and viscounts, the sons of fathers of the same rank. These people were *peers*, a word that means "on the same plane with." The peers occupied the only plane worth mentioning, the elevated plane, above the great many. The peers were arranged in a hierarchy, each proud of his rank, whatever it was, but also keen for a higher one. Their love for their own sons demanded it. The forms of address were carefully observed for all the ranks: your grace, your lordship, your ladyship.

In the best kingships there was scope for talent to rise, but not to the highest rank. In the late eighteenth century, the time of the American

Revolution, one could be pretty sure that the practices of Henry VIII would not return, but people knew what they were. Sir Thomas More was a friend, fellow student, and teacher of Henry VIII. More was a man from a middling family, born with genius of mind and character, and raised to a high place. He spent long evenings with the king in delightful conversation. He wrote great articles with him on matters of man and God. He and the king wrote in those articles that certain things must not be done, on peril of one's soul. More lived as few could imagine: he knew fame, wealth, and power; all looked to him with respect and nearly all with deference. Then the king who befriended him and raised him up to high places turned on him. Sir Thomas was imprisoned, starved, and deprived of books and warmth, and finally he was killed. This happened because Sir Thomas refused to do the very thing that he and the king had written would imperil their souls. The king presented him the terrible choice between duty to God and protection of family.

The case is not unique. Consider the ancestor of the statesman Winston Churchill, the general John Churchill, the scourge of Louis XIV, the founder of British greatness on the battlefield, made by Queen Anne the first Duke of Marlborough. Anne, John, and his wife, Sarah, were bosom friends when Anne was only an heir to the throne with little chance of occupying it. They were friends when their lives were at risk in dynastic struggles. They were friends when fate and fortune placed Anne on the throne, friends when she made him commander in the great war that embroiled all Europe, friends when he won every battle he fought for ten years, friends when he broke the French ambition to dominate Europe. Then, the day came that they were not friends, and soon Marlborough was not favored but dismissed, charges were brought, and he went into exile.

Queen Anne was a friend to Marlborough, and Henry VIII was a friend to Thomas More, so far as a monarch can be a friend to a regular man. That did not always prove to be so very far, and it did not always prove to last.

Great Britain in 1776 was an example of the moderate form of kingship. Like the best of the kings, George III, sovereign of the United Kingdom of Great Britain and Ireland, did not enjoy absolute power. In many ways he was a blessing to his people.

In his personal life, George was very concerned to place himself in the right and not to depend on his power alone. He was for a monarch humble, common, and dutiful. He began and ended each day in prayer and contemplation of Scripture. He urged his son to do the same. He was easy in contact even with ordinary people, when he had that contact. His faith taught him that even the "best of us are poor creatures."[1] He had such an interest in the practical side of agriculture, and such an ordinary and homely way of speaking of it, that he was often called "Farmer George."[2]

Ten years before Jefferson's Declaration was addressed to him, George III wrote for his son a defense of his conduct as king, in which he does not "pretend to superior abilities," but, he says, he gives place to no one in "meaning to preserve the freedom, happiness, and glory of my dominions, and all their inhabitants, and to fulfill the duty to my God and my neighbor in the most extended sense." He concludes: "That I have erred is undoubted, otherwise I should not be human, but I flatter myself that all unprejudiced persons will be convinced that whenever I have failed it has been from the head not the heart."[3]

The Declaration of Independence refers to George as a tyrant. No one who reads his letters can believe he thought or intended so. He does not justify himself, even in a private letter to his son and heir, on the ground of his own wishes. In some important sense, he regards himself as a servant. In his own eyes his kingship would not be legitimate except that it should serve the freedom and happiness of his dominions and their inhabitants, and also except that it should constitute a duty to God.

All that is on the one hand. On the other are the fact and nature of the kingship. George III lived in opulence and authority, and these benefits came to him personally because of how he was born. He rode in a carriage huge and dazzling. Wherever he went the people gaped, often in vast throngs whose joy was to catch a glimpse of him. He attended on his subjects frequently, but only those few who could afford the proper dress were able to approach him. He knew therefore only a few people of a certain kind; he required the support of fewer still. Each move of his body, each tic of his face, was studied to catch the least sign of his favor or disfavor.

When his son fell in love with a woman not of royal blood, he forbade the match; no prince should marry a subject, no matter if his heart commanded it.[4] To keep a clean heart is vital, George thought, but even a clean heart must not stoop below its station.

George III was referred to as "Majesty," a title of veneration from Rome through both the romantic and the Germanic languages. It refers to the dignity either of a god or of an exalted person, and so it associates the two. It was the habit of men in those days to think that God designated some men by birth to rule others. George the Farmer believed this with an unshakable conviction, and this conviction would make him do things that were repugnant to his colonies in America. Likely his intentions were as just as they could be, but still his actions amounted to expropriation, to arrest, to execution, to threats to families, including women and children. Sovereigns, whoever they are and whatever principle brings them to power, are likely to act this way when their sovereignty is at stake, a point well known to the Founders and affecting the way they wrote the Constitution. When the sovereign is an individual, and when he holds the sovereignty by a personal right, the problem can be worse.

This sense of majesty in the king was so strong that it was shared by nearly all of the colonists in America to some degree, and only a long series of tense and violent steps could efface it. Those steps began in 1763, when Britain won one of its several great wars with France. In Europe this war was called the Seven Years' War; in America, the French and Indian War. Now reaching a peak of strength, Britain began to take a closer interest in her colonies. She would tax and regulate them in new ways, and she would do it from Imperial London, now the center of the world. She would use part of this new money to pay for a new kind of administration, accountable not to those governed but to Imperial London. In other words, the colonists would pay for the officials sent to tell them what to do.[5]

Surprised and puzzled by the intrusion of British power into their familiar affairs, the colonists protested their loyalty to the king's sovereignty as loudly as they did their objections to his policy. Daniel Dulany, a Maryland lawyer who would not in the end support independence, was the kind of man easiest to follow in the beginning. Even in a letter of protest against the taxes from London in 1765, he wrote that "the colonies are dependent upon Great Britain, and the supreme authority vested in the King, Lords, and Commons, may justly be exercised to . . . preserve their Dependence, whenever necessary for that purpose."[6]

As late as July 8, 1775, a year before the Declaration, the colonies make a strong and official protest to the king in the form of the Olive Branch Petition.[7] It is signed by several of the eventual signers of the Declaration, including prominently John Hancock. It complains of the "irksome variety of artifices practiced by many of your Majesty's Ministers" and of their "delusive pretences, fruitless terrors, and unavailing severities." At the same time they profess themselves "attached to your Majesty's person, family, and Government, with all devotion that principle and affection can inspire."

This means that even here, in the New World, from which the Declaration of Independence would spring, the ground was not first broken with the intention of planting such a seed. Dulany insisted that the king's authority was limited, but admitted that the authority existed whether the people consented to it or not. This was simply the common sense of the matter, even in Great Britain, but even more so in other European countries where monarchs were generally stronger and more nearly absolute.

． ． ． ． ．

The Declaration of Independence does not read like a document from this world of kings. It hardly reads like a document from any particular world at all.

The first words of the Declaration are, "When in the Course of human events, it becomes necessary for one people . . ." This does not mean now, in North America in 1776, where killing has broken out between a long-settled government and the people. It does not mean the room in Philadelphia where the signers are gathered. The Declaration does not refer to any particular place. It does not mean those particular signers, either. It does not mean the people who elected those signers. The Declaration does not begin with any reference to those who write and ratify it, or to the nation they are forming.

If you think about it a minute, this will seem remarkable. At the time of the Declaration, armies are being formed, and people have been killed. Others have lost their property, and many more will do so. The signers of the Declaration acknowledge these obvious facts in the last sentence, when they mutually pledge "to each other" their lives, their fortunes, and their sacred honor. This is like a soldier's bond, each pledging to stand by the man next to him. Anyone can see how this kind of language would get into the Declaration of Independence. That is how people talk when they are risking their lives in war.

But what about this beginning, which is so abstract? The beginning treats these events not as something special or unique but as something that occurs "in the Course of human events." Soldiers who do brave acts are often shy about discussing them: "Anyone would have done the same." "I was very frightened, and I acted by instinct." This modesty is common from soldiers, especially when they are speaking to people who were not there with them. The modesty of the opening of the Declaration is rather like that. Its signers are at the crisis of their lives, and they begin by placing it in context. Because such things happen from time to time, there are standards according to which one must behave in them.

Having established that the situation is not without precedent, the Declaration turns to the standard according to which one must act in such situations. That standard is the "Laws of Nature and of Nature's God." Established in these laws is the principle of equality, first for peoples, who are entitled to a separate and equal station under these "Laws of Nature and of Nature's God." Also, each individual person is similarly entitled. This is established by a "self-evident" truth, that is, a truth whose proof is contained in the terms of the truth itself. If you know what a man is, you know that he is created equal. According to this self-evident truth, all men are "created equal," and "they are endowed by their Creator with certain unalienable Rights," among which are "Life, Liberty and the pursuit of Happiness." The purpose of government is "to secure these rights." This is the only reason stated why government is "instituted among Men." In all cases, government derives its "just powers from the consent of the governed."

These principles are not mere abstractions. They are introduced into a concrete situation, a situation established in a long history that includes the elevation and fall of Sir Thomas More and of the Duke of Marlborough, the high station of George III and his ancestors, the titles and privileges and courtesies of the court. These "Laws of Nature and of Nature's God" are therefore necessary to the situation. It is obvious that the Revolutionaries cannot appeal to the laws of Great Britain: the purpose of the document is to throw off those laws. It is obvious that they cannot appeal to their own opinions or wishes, unless they are megalomaniacs. Only of God can it be said that His will constituted a rule that all peoples, in all places, and at all times must obey. The Founders needed a law as universal as the circumstances the law is supposed to cover. They needed a law applicable in all nature.

The word *nature* has several meanings, two of which are most important here. The first is implicit in the origin of the word: *nature* comes from the Latin word for birth or to be born. Everything that is born is born something. In this sense, the nature of a thing is what that thing is, or whatever about that thing makes it what it is. For living things, this means their essential element—for example, the ability of human beings to reason and to talk. And nature is also the process of begetting and growth by which humans come to be—for example, that human babies are born to human parents and that they grow up within a certain range of time, age at a certain rate, die within a certain range of time, require a certain amount of rest and nourishment, and so on. In this sense, the nature of the thing describes for us just what it is and the main ways it goes about living.

The other use of the term *nature* is general: the nature of things, meaning all things. It is how things work. It means grand things, like the sun coming out and making warmth and day, and the sun going down and leaving night. It means small things like apples falling from the trees, and grand things like the gravity that pulls apples down. It means the dog wagging his tail when he is happy and growling when he is angry. It means the way of things.

If particular things have a nature, and if things in general have a nature, one can see how one might think that there are rules in nature. The rules would be the combination of the particular nature of each thing and the grand way that things work. These are the rules suggested by the expression the "Laws of Nature and of Nature's God." The great thinker Thomas Aquinas, following Aristotle and many others besides, defines the natural law as "the rational creature's participation of the eternal law."[8] By our rationality, we can see the laws of nature and of nature's God.

Another form of the word *rationality* is *reason*. It is the ability to reason that makes us able to understand the nature of things—both the specific nature that makes each thing what it is and the general workings of nature.

If you think about it, our ability to talk comes from this ability to see the nature of things: reason and speech are the same faculty. When we talk, we always have to use the common noun. There is a mystery hiding inside these nouns. It is very difficult to give an account of exactly how we use them. How do we know that a cup is a cup, when there are so many, and they are so different? Look at a few in your cupboard, and try to remember your parents or your teachers showing you pictures of them so you know what they are. Our teachers and our parents will have done that for just a few things, and yet we can recognize many, indeed we can recognize any. Also, when they did it, they were not teaching us that each thing fits into a kind; they were only teaching us the English names for the kind. Very small children seem to be able to tell a cow from a pig before they know the words *cow* and *pig*. Indeed, they seem to be able to associate a picture in two dimensions of a pig with a real pig, just as they can quickly associate the word *pig* with a real pig.

How do we humans do that? How do we know that a small pony is a horse and a Great Dane is a dog? That is a very difficult question to answer, every bit as difficult as it is easy for us to perform the feat. We humans recognize things in their categories, and we could not form a single sentence if we could not. Given this gift, we are able to talk.

This ability to talk places us in very close community with each other, much closer than other kinds of creatures. When you say that you "saw a beautiful canyon," you are conveying something meaningful even to a person who never saw a canyon and could not tell you quickly what beauty is. When you say, "I am married to a woman lovely and good," you are saying something meaningful to people who have never been married and who would struggle to tell you not only what loveliness is but also good. It is, in other words, the nature of man to reason and to speak. This capacity liberates us to understand and to choose, and also it connects us closely to each other. One of the many odd things about us is that we are at once free and independent, and also more closely connected than any other creatures found in nature.

The use of these common nouns also makes us judges of things in a different way than we would be if we did not have them. Dogs and cats have their likes and dislikes based simply on what instinct commands them or else what we train them to do. We humans carry around with us a standard of evaluation that is different from our wants and from our instincts. When we identify a thing as a cup, we recognize something that makes it a cup. It has about it the "good" of the cup in it. "Good and being are convertible terms," writes a philosopher.[9] And if we have a cup with a hole in the bottom, we recognize that it is not a very good cup. We could more likely use it for a funnel or a strainer, if we could use it all. As it loses the goodness of the cup, it loses also the being of the cup; it loses its "cupness." In a famous conversation in Jane Austen's *Pride and Prejudice*, Caroline says that a certain kind of party would be much more rational if there were conversation instead of dancing. Bingley replies, "Much more rational, my dear Caroline, I dare say, but it would not be near so much like a ball."[10] "Ball," then, is a thing we can recognize and call by a name. To be a ball, a thing must be in some sense a "good" ball; otherwise a conversation or a croquet match could be a ball.[11] To have the being of a thing is to have the good of it.

This word *good* takes on, then, a rich meaning, located somewhere near the center of our ability to see things for what they are and give names to them. And once we know that things fit in a category, we have automatically a standard by which to evaluate them against each other. Questions of good and bad, of right and wrong, of just and unjust, are written in our capacity with language. They are written in our nature. We have automatically a standard by which to evaluate one thing against another of its kind, the claim that one thing is good against the related claim of goodness by another thing of the same kind. We have naturally an acquaintance with the laws of nature and of nature's God, we have it without training, and we cannot resist awareness of it.

We can see two things. The first is that human beings have a unique ability, among earthly creatures, to perceive the natures of things, and this makes us aware of a rule or law or right of nature. The second is that the rational ability to make moral distinctions and the rational ability to speak bring human beings together in political communities. These communities concern the good and the bad, the just and the unjust, and all lawmaking involves precisely this sense of morality and justice.

. . . . .

Now, these things have been known for a long time, at least as long as the first philosophers in Greece, but really much longer than that. The Roman philosopher Cicero, a favorite of the Founders, writes, "[T]rue law is right reason, consonant with nature, spread through all people. It is constant and eternal."[12] Aristotle and Plato do not write of the natural law, but the standard of nature is the one to which they appeal in their analysis of particular political regimes and of particular political practices. Political philosophy is born in the idea that some truth may be found in the opinions about justice and injustice that are expressed in the law and in the claims of individual men and women.

These ideas are not only old; they are also widely known in every age either implicitly, through common sense, or explicitly, by thinking about it and putting the argument together. King George III himself manifested knowledge of these laws, even if he did not proclaim them. It stands to reason, one might say, that everyone has some knowledge of these laws, as is manifest in the ability of everyone to think and to speak.

That makes it all the more remarkable that the United States of America should be the first nation founded with an explicit statement of these laws. Alexander Hamilton writes beautifully that "the sacred rights of mankind are not to be rummaged for among old parchments. . . . They are written, as with a sun beam, in the whole volume of human nature by the hand of Divinity itself."[13] The whole volume of human nature has been around for a long time. Why, one might wonder, should the Declaration of Independence become the first parchment to reflect those laws? The answer has to do with the principle of equality and its effect when it is fully realized.

~⊸ FIVE ⊸~

THAT ALL MEN ARE
CREATED EQUAL

IF YOU ARE GOING TO DEFY THE MIGHTIEST EMPIRE ON earth, you might exercise a little caution. Especially if you have hardly any government and hardly any army, you might look for a way to appease. You might express the hope that the emperor keeps his power over everyone else, and not you. You might distinguish your case: our circumstances are special, and no other subjects of the emperor need follow us. If your potential allies, the nations that do not like your emperor, are also monarchies and aristocracies, you might assure them that you like their form of government just fine. Tell them to keep it. Tell the emperor only to leave you alone; say that you are no danger.

The Declaration of Independence does not adopt this tone. It begins:

> We hold these truths to be self-evident, that all men are cre-
> ated equal, that they are endowed by their Creator with certain

unalienable Rights, that among these are Life, Liberty and the pursuit of Happiness.—That to secure these rights, Governments are
instituted among Men, deriving their just powers from the consent
of the governed.

This idea of equality and consent of the governed seems to have
been important to the Founders. It mattered enough for them to flaunt
it before powerful adversaries who were likely to be inflamed by it, to
parade it before potential friends who were likely to be repelled. What
does it mean?

This is a hard question to answer because we are so obviously
not equal. Think of the differences among us. Some are qualified to
play offensive tackle in the NFL. To do this, one must be exceptionally
large, not to mention quick and strong enough to defend the blind
side against people also huge, strong, and swift. And among the small
subset of us who are so qualified, not all are excellent in mind and
character. Such men are few, and they are not "equal."

Or consider a young woman who is capable as an undergradu-
ate of producing original and important scholarship on Elizabethan
poetry. This would be another small subset among us. Add the attributes of beauty and moral virtue, and smaller still. Such a young
woman is not "equal."[1]

This is the rule you see everywhere, in common objects and
refined, in old things and new, in large things and small. Each individual thing is its own thing with its own qualities and capacities.

Take that ordinary object we mentioned in the last chapter, the cup.
Cups are all different, some widely so. There is the golden chalice, and
there is the upside-down paper cone beside the water cooler. The first is
sought through quests and valiant deeds related in story and song; the
second is used, crumpled, discarded, and forgotten. The two objects
are in these respects nearly opposite, as different as heavy and light, as
shining and dull, as precious and common, as lasting and ephemeral.
In these respects they are not equal. They are not even similar.

But then again, there is that one attribute in which the two objects are equal: they are both cups. It is actually easier to describe what makes the golden chalice special, or the paper cup common, than it is to describe what makes both of them cups. And yet to recognize the cup in each of them is a work of intuition that every rational creature performs instantly and without error. It seems that things can be equal without being similar. They can have the same nature despite wide variations in every accidental respect. This common nature is so obvious as to be the subject of propositions that are called "self-evident." If one understands the proposition, he sees the proof. All cups are created equal.

So are all men. It is "self-evident" that they are "created equal." And just as with cups, so with men their equality does not require that they are even similar in any respect except the essential ones. Our NFL player is very large and quick; most of us are much smaller and slower. Our young scholar has a gift for the use of words and the penetration of their meaning; most of us are not so facile. Yet he and she are men, which is to say human beings, and in that respect they are equal, both to each other and to us. The differences are very great in obvious physical and intellectual respects, and yet in essential respects they are nothing.

The essential similarity among humans may be harder to see when they are standing together, their differences manifest. It is easier to see when they are compared to something else. Such a comparison is right there in the Declaration of Independence, and we have already mentioned it. God is named four times in the Declaration. We can consider another human being both excellent and powerful, but we are not likely to think him the Creator, divine Providence, or the Supreme Judge of the World. We might think someone very fair and good, and we might trust that person's judgment implicitly. We are not likely to think him the very Author of the laws of nature and of nature's God.[2]

Some might think God an imaginary being and ask, what good is it to compare ourselves to something made up? The answer is that if God is an imaginary being, he is a being very easy to imagine. That is because we can see ourselves and the other creatures around us. If we can see what is different between a beast and a man, then it is not hard to imagine what would be the next step after man. If we can see inside ourselves which are the better and which the worse capacities, then we can imagine a being with only those better capacities.[3] If we can see that these better capacities that we possess are still imperfect in us, then we can imagine them perfected. Not only the Bible but also the classic authors conclude that nature points to the heavens.

Speaking of these other creatures, the beasts, they, too, help to display for us the nature of our equality (which is another way of saying the nature of our nature). We can compare ourselves to the beasts by observing them directly: they are here around us, sometimes too much around us. Anyone who travels on airplanes a lot will enjoy the story of a large pig being admitted to a seat on a flight from Philadelphia to Seattle. The owner of the pig allowed that the animal was her "therapeutic pet companion," and the poor gate agent acquiesced: the pig even got a ticket in first class. The pig did not act like the other passengers on the flight. There were snout marks on the windows. There were intrusions of the snout into people's laps. There was running up and down the aisle in squeals of panic in response to turbulence, accompanied by some incontinence. Neither the most nor the least remarkable human passenger on any airline flight could be mistaken for this pig. Compared to the pig, the most and the least remarkable among us look perfectly like the rest of us, that is, perfectly "equal."[4]

The pig, by the name of Charlotte, traveled on USAir on October 17, 2000. Her owner, a Ms. Andrews, denied that the pig was ill behaved. The Federal Aviation Administration said that it had no complaint to make about the presence of Charlotte. A spokesperson for USAir said pigs would no longer fly on that airline.

This distinction between man and God, on the one hand, and man and beast, on the other, underlies our political arrangements and has often emerged as the explicit basis of our policy. The pig himself has sometimes mattered. Abraham Lincoln had a series of debates with Stephen Douglas over the question of slavery and its growth into the "federal territories," the land belonging to the Union not yet incorporated as states. This was the specific point of issue that led to the Civil War. In one debate, Douglas argued that we can take our property, including our hog, into the Nebraska territory and the law will protect our ownership of it. Why not our slave? Lincoln replied,

> [I]nasmuch as you do not object to my taking my hog to Nebraska, therefore [you say] I must not object to you taking your slave. Now, I admit this is perfectly logical, if there is no difference between hogs and negroes. . . . I wish to ask whether you of the South yourselves, have ever been willing to do as much? . . . The great majority, South as well as North, have human sympathies, of which they can no more divest themselves than they can of their sensibility to physical pain. . . . In 1820 you joined the North, almost unanimously, in declaring the African slave trade piracy, and in annexing to it the punishment of death. Why did you do this? . . . The practice was no more than bringing wild negroes from Africa, to sell to such as would buy them. But you never thought of hanging men for catching and selling wild horses, wild buffaloes or wild bears.[5]

Lincoln argued that we manifest our knowledge of human equality even when we are cruel and unjust to one another. We always (except when we are simply insane) manifest some reservation or shyness about our actions. The Alabama slave code was a particularly harsh one. It contained restrictions on how long a slave could be indoors on another property than his owner's plantation, on how many slaves could gather and for how long, on the nature of the discussions they were permitted to have. But there were exemptions for some of these regulations for religious meetings. Those exemptions evince knowledge even among the slaveholders, even among those who supported the institution most strongly, of the humanity of the slaves.

Similarly the Nazis were more ready to work their atrocities on their victims than they were to talk about it candidly. For his part, Stalin admitted to Churchill that he killed millions of people but then went on to make a justification for doing it, a claim that some good would come to mankind because he did it.[6] The people he killed in this case were farmers, and he caused them to be starved to death. Even he saw that this was more controversial than killing the livestock that those farmers were tending.

. . . . .

Thomas Jefferson relied on the clarity of this comparison between man and beast in one of the last letters he ever wrote. It was written on June 24, 1826, ten days before the fiftieth anniversary of the Declaration of Independence and the day of Jefferson's death. Jefferson was writing to decline an invitation to the gala celebrations in Washington of that anniversary. His health would not permit him to go. And he added a little summary of the meaning of the Declaration:

> All eyes are opened, or opening, to the rights of man. The general spread of the light of science has already laid open to every view the palpable truth, that the mass of mankind has not been born with saddles on their backs, nor a favored few booted and spurred, ready to ride them legitimately, by the grace of god.[7]

A man may ride a horse and tell him where to go without violating the rights of the horse because he does not thereby interfere (so long as he does not abuse the horse) with any natural property of the horse. The horse does not choose as a human chooses: he will obey his instinct, or he will obey his master. He does not carry responsibility for his actions in the way that humans do precisely because he does not have the gift of reason. Reason displays to us the things in their kinds, and also the implications of better and worse that are apparent in them. Reason permits us to weigh means and ends, and to choose the one for the sake of the other. The rational being lives in a rich moral universe, populated with good and bad, right and wrong. Horses do not.

This gift of reason is not only the basic ground of human equality; it is also the ground of all rightful authority or governance. It is not only that men may rule beasts because they are rational and beasts are not; it is also that the rational parts of the human being are equipped, and therefore entitled, to govern the nonrational parts. The Constitution of the United States is written with a view to this distinction. It seeks to encourage the right ordering of the body politic along the lines of the right ordering of the soul. This is crucial precisely because the Constitution steadfastly refrains from placing any authority over people outside their consent.

Now, you may think that if reason is the title to rule, then the most rational person should be the ruler. There is something to this. The authority of parents over children stems in part from the fact that the children have not yet fully succeeded to their rational abilities. It cannot be denied that George Washington was better equipped, not only by his reason but also by the sum of all his virtues, to be president than most people, including most people who have been president. Why does it not then follow that possession of virtue gives one authority to rule? Why should the less virtuous have to consent before they are ruled? Why do governments derive "their just powers from the consent of the governed"? Why should not philosophers rule?

The answer has to do with the whole of our nature. It is true that we are the only creatures with the gift of reason. It is also true that in other respects we are like the animals. We have bodies and needs, and therefore we have interests. We have both pleasures and pains, and these are more acute in us than in animals that are not reasonable: other animals do not have a critical distance from what is happening to them, whereas we have immortal souls. We know our mortality through these immortal souls; we feel it acutely as we age. Therefore our wants and passions that go with our needs are powerful. Our passions provide a fuel or motive force for our actions; we need them, and the information they give us contains a lot of truth, but they can get out of hand.

Moreover, our reason is imperfect, in part because it is connected to our passions, in part because it does not see clearly. We can see this within ourselves because sometimes we can think more clearly than we can at others. Also, we converse with people who are especially good at reasoning. We find such people delightful, and yet even these people make mistakes and are not always at their best. This is one reason why it is easy for us to imagine what God or angels may be like. Just think of someone who is always as well ordered and clear-seeing as you are at your best moment, and yet that person can see and comprehend all, which you can never do. You are building up a picture of something divine.

Also, every human being, whatever his capacity (except in those rare cases where his reason is entirely disabled by illness or other condition), possesses within himself the ability to direct himself and his labor, to provide for himself and his loved ones. This is essentially connected to the gift of reason, and the requirement to use it is essentially connected to the fact of our being animals, animals with reason and also animals with bodies. To take this from us is to take something that is every bit as much a natural property as our reason.

The great majority of us will never make any money playing NFL football, which requires gifts we do not have, as well as massive labor that speaks of many qualities of character. These things are the football player's own, born in him and developed by his life's labor. He must decide, along the course of his career, many difficult things: whether to accept a further contract, when the time comes, with the team for which he plays. If he refuses it, he might get a bigger one later, or he might get hurt and lose the chance. These risks are his own, and the mind to think about them is his own, and therefore the choice is his own. No one has the right to make it for him.

Similarly with the young scholar: How will she balance the love of learning and teaching with her desire to be a wife and mother? These are her own choices to make as well.

This is what James Madison means by the "diversity in the faculties of man, from which the rights of property originate."[8] We are born with needs, and we are born with faculties with which to supply those needs. As the needs are ours, and the faculties are ours, so the deployment of the faculties is ours. Abraham Lincoln described the relationship between our reason, our needs, and our labors with his beautiful common poetry at a Wisconsin fair:

> Free Labor argues that, as the Author of man makes every individual with one head and one pair of hands, it was probably intended that heads and hands should cooperate as friends; and that that particular head, should direct and control that particular pair of hands. As each man has one mouth to be fed, and one pair of hands to furnish food, it was probably intended that that particular pair of hands should feed that particular mouth—that each head is the natural guardian, director, and protector of the hands and mouth inseparably connected with it; and that being so, every head should be cultivated, and improved, by whatever will add to its capacity for performing its charge. In one word Free Labor insists on universal education.[9]

Wisdom is worth something, it is true. But according to Lincoln's simple observation of the nature of man, even the wisest man has interests of his own, having a mouth of his own to feed. These interests will not be exactly the same as those of others. And even if his wisdom is great, it is not as great at one time as it is at another. This means that his wisdom alone, given the whole of his nature, cannot give him a title to govern, unless the governed give their agreement. Otherwise, he would be taking something from others that belongs to them, and he would be doing so without any assurance that he will behave as an angel might behave exercising such authority. For that reason, human beings must hold the means of their well-being in their own hands. This is the reason that government must be limited, so that we in private society may do that.

. . . . .

The necessity of government by consent is written, therefore, in the fact of human equality. That is also the basis for limited government. The very reason we have constitutional rule has to do with the fact that we are neither angels nor beasts, but in between the two. Think again about this statement by James Madison:

> It may be a reflection on human nature that such devices should be necessary to control the abuses of government. But what is government itself but the greatest of all reflections on human nature? If men were angels, no government would be necessary. If angels were to govern men, neither external nor internal controls on government would be necessary.[10]

Equality, we can see, is essential to comprehending nature as the Founders conceived it. Also, government by consent is a necessary deduction from the equality of men in nature. To the Founders, these ideas are inseparable. Today, they have been separated in our understanding.

The idea of nature, as the Founders used it, is not so popular among us today as it was in their time. Especially is this true among the extensively educated. We tend not to imagine a world populated by abiding things, things with a nature, so much as a world of transient things. We tend to think things evolve, and to think this process of evolution or development to be the fundamental fact; the one abiding fact is that nothing abides. This difference is somewhere near the heart of our difference with the Founders and with most of human thinking before them.

Because the idea of nature in the Founding and the idea of equality in the Founding are so connected as to trace their source to the same place, it would seem to follow that we today must not like the idea of equality any better than we like the idea of nature. But this is not true: we like equality very much. It is the touchstone of American politics today as much as ever it was. But that is possible only because its meaning has been adjusted, and this adjustment is the chief reason for the changes in our politics. Today we think of equality as an outcome, something that comes about as a result of activity both personal and political, rather than the condition under which our actions begin and operate. Equality is now a thing that we can make.

There are powerful arguments to support this idea. First of all, there is the downside of the old idea of equality—namely, inequality. If we mean by inequality the enjoyment by some of luxury amidst idleness, and the privation of others amidst toil and trouble, then no one likes that, likely not even the rich. If we mean by inequality that a man must have two jobs, and his wife two jobs as well, and still have trouble supporting their children, no one likes that. If we mean by it that workers are hungry while the bosses are fat, no one likes that. If we mean by it that some identifiable group, marked out by the color of skin or the source of ancestry, has relatively little, while other groups so identified have more, we all feel ashamed of that. If that is inequality, then the cure is equality. We should make people more equal. That is the equality we think of today.

The modern argument, the argument of the "Progressives," is that the Founders' idea of equality is not superseded, but transcended, by events. In their day inequality came in the form of the king, born to rule, and his nobles, born to help him. They had the dominant place in politics and the economy. Now things have changed, and both the danger and the opportunity are different. Now the spread of freedom has done just what James Madison said it would do: it has liberated some of us to prosper, and we have set ourselves up in fine style. And once we have arrived at the pinnacle, we take all kinds of actions to keep others below us. Now we do not have kings and royalty, but we have something else: "royalists of the economic order"[11] and "malefactors of great wealth."[12] The concentration of wealth that they command threatens the whole economy because if something is not done, there will be no consumers left to buy the things that workers make, and then there will be no jobs, and then there will be no profits for the factory owners, and finally we will all end up in a common destruction.

Progressives argue also that we cannot really have the security of our property unless all of us guarantee the property of one another. If we live in peril of our livelihoods, then all of our freedoms are compromised. "Necessitous men are not free men."[13] Also: "the political equality we once had won was meaningless in the face of economic inequality." In the face of the new economic threats, American citizens "could only appeal to the organized power of government."[14] "In our day these economic truths have become accepted as self-evident. We have accepted, so to speak, a Second Bill of Rights."[15] These words were written during and just after the Great Depression. Surely government has to become more involved in the economy and other parts of society to prevent such crises.

Many events, including the Great Depression, revealed to the new Progressive thinkers that through the evolution of time, there is an evolution of rights. Unless we keep up with that evolution, and even begin to shape that evolution, we will be overcome and lose all rights. It is the job of government, they believe, to protect equality through new measures to guarantee that the results of economic competition do not get out of hand. It is a powerful and persuasive argument, and it has remade the workings of our government to a place almost beyond recognition.

It had to be this way, argue the new thinkers, because times have changed. It is the way of times to change, and the Founders were wrong to think they do not. The kind of government they built is not adaptable to the new circumstances, so we have to change it. In particular, we have to organize government to be more active in more ways, and also it must be more scientifically based. In fact, we have to invent a new kind of government system, the very "fourth branch" that Professor Klarman from chapter two likes so well. This new branch will be able to perform all kinds of wonderful things because of its training. Also, it will be wholly focused on the public good because it will operate quite outside politics and beyond political control, and also because its members will be safe in their jobs. If you give people permanent employment and good salaries, they will not want anything else. They will not pursue their own interests because all their interests are satisfied. They will get along with one another very well because they will run a unified system; legislative, executive, and judicial powers will be rolled into a single agency.[16] It is, in a certain way, an emulation of the divine governance of the universe, except it will be done by men.

This is the origin of the entitlement state and the administrative system that goes with it. Built on a different understanding of nature, of equality, and of consent, it proposes different policies and different ways of pursuing them. It sets out to solve the problems of want, misfortune, and injustice in the society. It holds out the great hope of a planned and rational society, in which none need suffer unduly and all who suffer will have relief. These are the new self-evident truths it has discovered.

. . . . .

I have not set out here to make the case about the consequences of these policies. They are evident everywhere. No one today argues seriously that the administrative state in Washington, which is of unprecedented size and still growing, is neutral about politics, as was intended. Some think its political influence is for good, and some do not. Some think that the great achievements of desegregation and the social safety net are attributable to this system. Some deny that and think that the breakdown of the family and the growth of a chronic underclass are its children. Some think it has made us rich; some, that it has made us broke. We will not settle that here, or in any book, but in the court of public opinion, that highest tribunal on earth.

The first step is to be aware of the contrast between the two views of equality and the two views of rights. They are not compatible. One or the other must be chosen. There is no halfway house between them.

The Founders' view holds that nature, equality, and consent speak with a single voice and even, because they require and include each other, in a single word. The more modern or Progressive view thinks them severed: nature is an outmoded idea, which means that it was never a true idea. Consent must be relaxed in the name of equality: we can all come out well if we give a greater power to the government to act unfettered. Equality is a construct. Any group may identify itself as oppressed, and the feeling of oppression is powerful evidence for the claim. Above all, equality has to do with outcomes. The "different and unequal faculties of acquiring property" must be suppressed or channeled by the government into productive avenues in order to bring about the desired outcomes.[17]

The Founders thought that all our rights are connected. Our right to property is based on the same facts as our freedom of speech. Our right to the material things that we earn is founded in the same nature as our freedom to worship and pray as we please. Our civil and political rights depend on our ability to hold the means of our well-being in our own hands. We can have no rights of any kind that do not leave "to everyone else the like advantage."[18] This means that nothing properly called a right takes anything from anyone else.

The Progressives think that we must surrender title to our property into a common pool so that all can have their property guaranteed. They think that our civil rights are now long since assured, and can even be regulated, in order to make sure we live better and more harmoniously together.[19]

The Founders thought that the government must rest entirely on public opinion. They thought the powers of government, and also the influence of people on the government, must be organized through forms that restrain as they empower, elevate as they license. The Progressives think that a new kind of administration, built in part on the sovereignty of scientific knowledge and practices, could solve the problems of society in ways that have never been known. This kind of government must above all be empowered to act. Form must give way to function.

The Founders thought that the greatest effort in relief of poverty in human history is the building of a free republic, protecting equally the right to property and resting on consent through a free Constitution. They thought that this would give rise to a system of local government, run mainly by volunteers, that would be involved in every kind of relief of the needy. They thought that churches and other philanthropies would flourish in aid of those who fell behind. They thought that people would grow in the strength and practice of self-government to be as good as people can be.[20] They thought that universal education, run like every other matter of domestic administration—without bureaucracy or central control—would help to provide the ideal of the first free nation on earth. Lincoln, a great student of the Revolution, would call this "an open field and a fair chance" to all.[21]

The Progressives think the Founders' system imperfect. The Founders thought so too. Men, they thought, are not angels. They can live well and freely, but this is not heaven.

~~ SIX ~~

HYPOCRISY

IT IS ALL WELL AND GOOD TO FLING HIGH TALK ABOUT
equal rights before a mighty king. But what about you, you Founders?
Did you respect the rights of others in the way that you demanded the
king respect yours?

The Declaration of Independence and the Constitution of the
United States were made by a people who were slaveholders, and within
the Constitution are three provisions that recognize and protect the
institution of human slavery.[1] The authors of both the Declaration of
Independence and the Constitution included buyers, owners, and sell-
ers of slaves. Among the slaveholders were three of the most prominent
of the Founders: George Washington, James Madison, and Thomas
Jefferson. Of these only Washington liberated his slaves, which he did
only upon his death. How can we excuse this?

Begin with the fact that the Founders placed themselves in
an interesting *ad hominem* position by writing the Declaration of
Independence in the way that they did. They were acutely aware of the

contradiction between the principles of the Declaration and the fact that they owned other people. They could expect criticism based on these principles, and sure enough that criticism was quick to come. It came from an official source—the British administration to which the Declaration was addressed.

The British administration, led at that moment by Lord North, encouraged a lawyer in London by the name of John Lind to reply.[2] Most of his reply is about the list of charges against the king and Parliament that make up the main body of the document. This middle part of the Declaration, the part after the universal opening, was at the time the most noticed and important part. According to the Declaration, it supplies the facts ("let Facts be submitted to a candid world") that justify the colonists in exercising their natural right to form their own nation. The British were eager to refute these charges and spent most of their time on them.

Lind makes reference to the opening passages of the Declaration. He reminds the colonists, now Americans, that this high-blown talk about equal rights and government by consent sounds very pretty coming from a bunch of slaveholders, especially when it is addressed to a mother country in which there are no slaves. In response to the twenty-seventh charge brought against the king ("He has excited domestic insurrections amongst us"), Lind writes:

> But how did his Majesty's Governors excite domestic insurrections? . . . [T]hey offered freedom to the slaves of these assertors of liberty. . . . Is it for them to say, that it is tyranny to bid a slave to be free? To bid him take courage, to rise and assist in reducing his tyrants to a due obedience to law? To hold out as a motive to him, that the load which crushed his limbs shall be lightened; that the whip which harrowed up his back shall be broken, that he shall be raised to the rank of a freeman and a citizen? It is their boast that they have taken up arms in support of these their own self-evident

truths—"that all men are equal"—"that all men are endowed with the unalienable rights of life, liberty, and the pursuit of happiness." Is it for them to complain of the offer of freedom held out to these wretched beings? of the offer of reinstating them in that equality, which, in this very paper, is declared to be the gift of God to all; in those unalienable rights, with which, in this very paper, God is declared to have endowed all mankind?[3]

According to Lind, the colonists are the tyrants, and the king and his administration are the force for liberty. He was able to claim this by the existence of slavery in the colonies and on the plantations of the very signers (and also the conflict with the Indian tribes). He was able to shame them with their own principles. He was able to hurl their charges back upon them redoubled. Unwilling to grant the principle that he could govern them only with their consent, the king was able still to appeal over their heads to the liberty of their slaves. It was for the Founders a terrible contradiction affecting the very ground upon which they stood.

There are plenty of problems with this claim from Lind. In fact, the British government had not been the consistent defender of liberty that Lind claims. Slavery had come to America under British law. British law permitted and also protected the slave trade in the British Empire until March 1807, three weeks after it was abolished in the United States.[4] Slavery itself was not abolished in the British Empire until 1833, thirty-two years before it was abolished in the United States, after a generation of campaigning by William Wilberforce and his colleagues in the abolition movement. British laws guaranteed that British ships would carry all trade, including slaves, in the West Indies. British ships transported about 3.5 million slaves to the New World, and that formed much of the economic basis of the British Empire in the West Indies, the most lucrative part of the empire. As regards slavery, there were many dirty hands in many countries.[5]

Yet these words from Lind must, as we say, have hurt. The Founders must have known that they were going to hear such words, and they must have known that they were going to hurt. That is because they said the same kinds of words against themselves, often and consistently. If a hypocrite is a man who pretends to virtues he does not have, the Founders were not that.

. . . . .

Take the case of Thomas Jefferson. Jefferson drafted a passage for the Declaration that condemned the king for the "execrable commerce" of the slave trade, which passage was deleted from the final version.[6] Jefferson was a participant in that "execrable commerce," a buyer and seller in that market. Moreover, there is a chance that he himself fathered a child by a slave, a beautiful young woman by the name of Sally Hemings, who cannot have had a free choice in the matter.[7] How can Jefferson have justified this?

The answer is that he did not justify it; he condemned it. Also he attempted to bring it to an end. Most effectively, he opposed slavery in the matter of Virginia's claims to western lands. Upon the urging of Jefferson, Virginia ceded its claims to those lands to the federal government. This set the pattern for the growth of the Union, not by accretions of territory to the existing states, but by the addition of new states on an equal footing with the old. The pattern is the opposite of colonial growth and the first example of the expansion of a free and representative government by adding additional free and representative citizens and states.

Jefferson also urged Virginia to cede its western claims with the condition that no slavery be permitted in those territories. This condition is recognized in the beautiful and famous Northwest Ordinance of 1787, which was for many decades listed in the US Code as the third "Organic Law" of the United States.[8] It provided the mechanism by which the western lands of the United States could be organized into territories, and then the territories organized into states. Article 6 of the Northwest Ordinance contains the following passage on slavery:

> There shall be neither slavery nor involuntary servitude in the said territory, otherwise than in the punishment of crimes whereof the party shall have been duly convicted: Provided, always, That any person escaping into the same, from whom labor or service is lawfully claimed in any one of the original States, such fugitive may be lawfully reclaimed and conveyed to the person claiming his or her labor or service as aforesaid.[9]

This sets a pattern to which Abraham Lincoln would later appeal in his famous Peoria speech. By the time Lincoln had entered politics, a movement had grown up to justify the institution of slavery, and this movement demanded the expansion of slavery into the western lands. Lincoln begins his great proof that the Founders were opposed to slavery with this provision of the Northwest Ordinance and its evidence of the opinions of Thomas Jefferson.[10]

Jefferson's most famous statement on slavery is in his book *Notes on the State of Virginia*, written in 1781–82. He writes:

> The whole commerce between master and slave is a perpetual exercise of the most boisterous passions, the most unremitting despotism on the one part, and degrading submissions on the other. . . . The man must be a prodigy who can retain his manners and morals un-depraved by such circumstances. And with what execration should the statesman be loaded, who permitting one half the citizens thus to trample on the rights of the other, transforms those into despots, and these into enemies, destroys the morals of the one part, and the *amor patriae* of the other. . . . And can the liberties of a nation be thought secure when we have removed their only firm basis, a conviction in the minds of the people that these liberties are of the gift of God? That they are not

to be violated but with his wrath? Indeed I tremble for my country when I reflect that God is just: that his justice cannot sleep for ever: that considering numbers, nature and natural means only, a revolution of the wheel of fortune, an exchange of situation, is among possible events: that it may become probable by supernatural interference! The Almighty has no attribute which can take side with us in such a contest.[11]

These are forecasts of doom. In the Declaration Jefferson appealed on behalf of the Americans to the "Supreme Judge of the World" for the rectitude to their intentions. He knew at the time what he made more explicit in the *Notes*—that the "Almighty has no attribute" that could side with them in the contest between the master and the slave. This means that the liberty of all is threatened by the oppression of some. In that, he portends the terrible judgment acknowledged by Abraham Lincoln in his Second Inaugural Address eighty-three years later:

> Yet, if God wills that [the war] continue until all the wealth piled by the bondsman's two hundred and fifty years of unrequited toil shall be sunk, and until every drop of blood drawn with the lash shall be paid by another drawn with the sword, as was said three thousand years ago, so still it must be said "the judgments of the Lord are true and righteous altogether."[12]

Few match the eloquence of Jefferson or Lincoln, but the record of the Founding is replete with such statements by its leading figures.[13]

The contradiction between the beliefs of Jefferson and his actions constitutes testimony of a peculiar and powerful kind to the influence of these "Laws of Nature and of Nature's God." Obviously the contradiction means that those laws are not everywhere obeyed. Thomas Jefferson, who wrote down the reference to them in the Declaration, did not obey them. And yet still he wrote them down. Somehow they were drawing him. He, a slaveholder, could not resist their attraction.

. . . . .

The Founders knew that the Declaration would build pressure to abolish the practice of slavery. They felt that pressure already, and they began to act on that pressure in ways that substantially reduced and restricted the practice of slavery in early America. One may blame them for the insufficiency of this. One may criticize them for removing from the Declaration the language against slavery that Jefferson proposed. One may say that they did not mean the principle of equality that they did place there. But why then should they place it there at all?

In a work of the first importance for understanding the Founding, Thomas West traces the steps taken to abolish slavery in most of the Union during the Revolutionary period. When the controversy with Great Britain began, slavery was legal in all parts of the colonies. He summarizes the steps:

> The third charge against the Founders was that they failed to abolish slavery. Our answer, to this point, has been: they limited and eventually outlawed the importation of slaves from abroad; they abolished slavery in a majority of the original states; they forbade the expansion of slavery into areas where it had not been previously permitted; they made laws regulating slavery more humane; individual owners in most states freed slaves in large numbers. In light of all this, it is a gross exaggeration to speak . . . of "the unfree origins of the United States." Freedom was secured for the large majority of Americans, and important actions were undertaken in the service of freedom for the rest.[14]

John Jay was one of the three authors of the *Federalist*, a diplomat, a governor of New York, and the first Chief Justice of the Supreme Court. He was a tireless worker for abolition. In June 1788 he wrote a letter to the president of the English Society for the Manumission of Slaves. In it, he explains the difficulty of abolition during the Revolution and the steady pressure that built for it. When the Revolution commenced, "the great body of our people had been so long accustomed to the practice and convenience of having slaves, that very few among them even doubted the propriety and rectitude of it." Then "liberal and conscientious men" began to draw the lawfulness of slavery into question. "Their doctrines prevailed by almost insensible degrees." They were like "the little lump of leaven which was put into three measures of meal." Even at the time he was writing, the "whole mass is far from being leavened, though we have good reason to hope and believe that if the natural operations of truth are constantly watched and assisted, but not forced and precipitated," then abolition can be achieved. "Many of the legislators in different states are proprietors of slaves," and therefore a "total and sudden stop to this species of oppression is not to be expected."[15]

Jay himself kept up this pressure throughout his career. He personally applied the pressure of principle upon the practices of his country. These practices had been long established, and they gave way slowly. The ideas adopted in the Founding were making demands through the agency of John Jay and people like him, and those demands were being heard.

. . . . .

Two generations later, the United States would suffer its most costly war over this issue of slavery. The Civil War arose from the question whether slavery would be extended across the whole continent, or whether it would be restricted and placed, as Lincoln said, "in the course of ultimate extinction." Lincoln believed the "real issue in this controversy . . . is the sentiment on the part of one class that looks upon the institution of slavery as a wrong, and another class that does not look upon it as a wrong."[16] Apparently something had interrupted the process of influence that John Jay described, the process leavening the whole mass of the people with the principles of liberty and equality. It is worth saying what that something is.

The apostle of proslavery sentiment is the thinker John C. Calhoun. He believed it an abomination for blacks and whites to live together as equal citizens. Unlike anyone in the classical world, he espoused a racial theory of inferiority. Such thinking is unknown to the American Revolution. Also, he based his theory significantly on the hopes and tenets of modern science. Writing on discoveries and inventions in his magnum opus, *Disquisition on Government*, he explained:

> When the causes now in operation have produced their full effect, and inventions and discoveries shall have been exhausted—if that may ever be—they will give a force to public opinion, and cause changes, political and social, difficult to be anticipated. What will be their final bearing, time only can decide with any certainty. That they will, however, greatly improve the condition of man ultimately—it would be impious to doubt.[17]

For Calhoun, piety and science come together to predict progress. Our human faculties, a gift from God, can be used over time only in support of good. Therefore the inferior must be subordinated to the superior among humans, so as not to obstruct this progress. Slavery is built then on the hierarchy of race that seems to Calhoun natural or inevitable among men, and the hierarchy is necessary to the advance of mankind toward its goal.[18] The process of scientific improvement will be our creation, but also it will work upon us, "give a force to public opinion, and cause changes, political and social." Holding these principles, Calhoun had to reject the principles of the Declaration.

Alexander Stephens, the vice president of the Confederacy, would extend Calhoun's reading of American history. Stephens quotes Jefferson that slavery was the "rock upon which the old Union would split." He was correct about this, Stephens thinks. The prevailing ideas entertained by Jefferson "and most of the leading statesmen at the time of the formation of the old Constitution" believed that the "enslavement of the African was in violation of the laws of nature; that it was wrong in principle, socially, morally, and politically." They did not know how to deal with this evil, but the "general opinion of the men of that day was that, somehow or other in the order of Providence, the institution would be evanescent and pass away." This is just what the Founders themselves said.

But they were wrong, according to Stephens, that slavery would pass away because they were wrong that slavery was wrong. The Confederacy is the first "in the history of the world, based upon this great physical, philosophical, and moral truth" of the good of slavery. It is a "discovery in the various departments of science." It is a truth "slow in development, as all truths are and ever have been, in the various branches of science." It is like the principles of astronomy announced by Galileo, or like the principles of political economy announced by Adam Smith. In the past, many governments have subordinated certain classes of the same race: this is "in violation of the laws of nature." In the Confederacy, all of the white race, "however high or low, rich or poor, are equal in the eye of the law." Not so with the "Negro": "Subordination is his place. He, by nature, or by the curse against Canaan, is fitted for that condition which he occupies in our system."[19]

Progressive and developmental thinking of a scientific nature has for Stephens revealed a new truth. It is a racial truth. It is wedded to his religion, a point to which Lincoln would respond: "[I]t may seem strange that some men should dare to ask a just God's assistance in wringing their bread from the sweat of other men's faces."[20]

In these respects, the Confederacy is a harbinger of a new political doctrine that would appear in virulent forms in Europe and also in the United States, especially in the twentieth century. According to this doctrine, not nature but history is the determinant of all things, including the status and even the consciousness of human beings. The ways of history are revealed to us in the discoveries of modern science. These discoveries show us the contingency of our own understanding, but also they give us a tool by which we can conquer, or anyway become the makers of, the forces of history. In Calhoun and Stephens, these doctrines are wedded to their understanding of religion; in later articulations they become the enemy of and the replacement for religion. The old liberalism of the American Revolution respected in principle the liberty of all, and it led our nation away from the practice of slavery. The new doctrines of history respect in principle the liberty of none, and they lead away from the practice of freedom.

Abraham Lincoln, whose statesmanship is part of the redemption found in the Civil War, suggested how we might think about our principles and the fact that we fail perfectly to follow them:

> [The authors of the Declaration of Independence] did not mean to assert the obvious untruth, that all were then actually enjoying that equality, nor yet, that they were about to confer it immediately upon them. In fact they had no power to confer such a boon. They meant simply to declare the right, so that the enforcement of it might follow as fast as circumstances should permit. They meant to set up a standard maxim for free society, which should be familiar to all, and revered by all; constantly looked to, constantly labored for, and even though never perfectly attained, constantly approximated, and thereby constantly spreading and deepening its influence, and augmenting the happiness and value of life to all people of all colors everywhere.[21]

Lincoln reminds us that the principles of right will among human beings be "never perfectly attained." He reminds us also that the pursuit of them will yield the best benefits that human life can afford. This was the direction of the American Revolution. The interruption of that movement has come not from service to the principles and institutions of the Revolution but from their abandonment.

SEVEN

THE MARRIAGE OF MANY CAUSES

NOW WE MUST THINK MORE SPECIFICALLY ABOUT CONSTI-
tutions. In one way, the questions about constitutions are hardest
because constitutions provide the form according to which the law is
shaped, and the law is nothing less than the most forceful of human
influences. When we discuss a constitution, we reach the place where
orders are given that must be obeyed upon pain of human compulsion.
We reach the proximate authority for all such orders.

What is the place of a constitution? A constitution is something
different from the Declaration of Independence, so grand in its
phrases, providing a purpose and a guide for the operation of a government, but not arranging the processes by which it operates. It is
something different from the regular ordinances of governments local
and national, different also from the rulings of a court or the actions
of an executive, different from the elections and appointments that put
officers in place. A constitution differs from other human laws in its
generality and supremacy. It differs from those ultimate laws named

in the Declaration, those "Laws of Nature and of Nature's God," in its particular and binding application on a people that has adopted it. It is somewhere between these things. It forms a bridge between them.

A constitution is not only described in the Declaration of Independence; it is necessary to it. The Declaration claims that the people may not be governed except when they have given their consent. They must agree that some particular offices must be occupied by some particular people who may do some particular things. The Declaration describes what kinds those offices ought to be and how they should be related to one another, but it does not provide the offices themselves or any way for their occupants to be selected. A constitution like the one we have is then a necessary element of the American government.

Think of the Founding of America as a work of art, in fact as a statue, something sculpted and made by the art and hands of a man. A constitution is the highest kind of *statute*, which means "law." It is no coincidence that the word *constitution*, the word *statute*, and the word *statue* are connected from ancient sources through the idea of setting a thing firmly in place or setting an imposing thing in place upon a firm basis.

The Founding of the United States is, more than any other parallel event in history, a work of art. Of course there were chance events of huge significance. Of course there were doubts and disagreements, misinformation and ignorance plaguing all the key actors in the drama. Still the key actions of the Founding were deliberately chosen through a process of debate, conducted by officers who had been selected by the people to do what they did. In this debate reasons were given pro and con, then decisions reached and reasons given for the decisions. We have therefore the speeches and the deeds in close association. There had never been anything like it, and it is hard to see how it can ever recur. Even when the speeches are in error, even when they are deceitful, we have the precious opportunity to compare them with one another and with the deeds to which they give rise or from which they proceed.

The Declaration of Independence and the Constitution are the prime examples of this pattern, and as the prime examples occurring amidst these unique events of the American Revolution, there is nothing quite like them in the history of the world. They are the products of careful crafting, and they state specific reasons for the decisions they represent. The fact that these decisions have proved to be monumental in scale and longevity makes it hardly credible that they were chosen for reasons that can be traced, and yet manifestly they were. The Declaration of Independence is little else than a list of the reasons why it came to be. The Constitution gave rise to a debate full of reasons pro and con, and several documents in that debate are among the most profound political statements in history. The Declaration of Independence and the Constitution were both surrounded by debate and disagreement, and yet both were adopted, and both are still in force two centuries later and more. The debate reached a decision, and the decision still stands, even if the ground beneath it has sometimes shaken and even if it shakes now.

. . . . .

What are the factors that made the Constitution possible? We might as well ask, what makes a statue possible? To begin with, there must be material, say marble. The final result depends very much on the material. A bronze statue looks different from a marble one, even if they have the same form, and a plastic statue looks different still. The equivalent in the making of America would be the people of the nation and the land upon which they live. Just as the marble in the statue, so the people and the place of the United States have an effect on the nature of the country. In the first *Federalist*, Hamilton says that it is reserved to "the people of this country" to decide for all time "whether societies of men are really capable or not of establishing governments by reflection and choice."[1] Madison refers to the "genius" of the American people.[2] This people had lived a certain way and learned certain things. They were different from other peoples. Because of them and other factors, the country was, and I argue still is, different from other countries. The difference between one people and another is of essential importance. Still, it is not the only difference between countries, just as the differences in the material are not the only differences in a statue.

Someone must work on the material to make it into an artifact; that is what art means. Sculptors make statues, and the sculptor matters very much to the outcome. In Rome and Florence there are several statues by Michelangelo. It is worth the journey to those cities just to see those statues, even if one ignores the other wonders there. The sublime and tragic gentleness of his *Pieta* can be compared to the gravity and potency of his *Moses*. His *David* is massive and yet perfectly poised, a picture of human beauty befitting, if a man could make anything so, an image of one chosen directly by God. The people who can make works of art so wonderful are "much rarer than the largest and purest diamonds."[3] What can we say of the people who made and justified the Declaration of Independence and the Constitution of the United States? These documents have many critics today. What have the critics done to match them? It matters very much that it was Michelangelo who set out to make the *David*. It matters very much that George Washington, Thomas Jefferson, and James Madison lived and worked during the American Revolution. Ours would be a different nation without them.

Works of art are made for a reason. Something moves the artist. It is so hard to make any work of art, and the difficulty is much greater than simply the hard work of carving and shaping stone or of forging metal. A work of art must live in the mind of the artist, and human beings are so contrived that a great thing in their minds places a strain upon their bodies too. No one can read the life of Michelangelo without seeing the cost he paid to produce what he produced.[4] Neither can anyone miss the fire in the hearts of those who made the United States, those who pledged their lives, their fortunes, and their sacred honor. It was not

just risk of death and dishonor: it was also years of anxious calcula-
tion amidst unknowns; it was responsibility for things they could not be
certain to control; it was the burden of carrying the hopes of millions.
What called this forth from them? The sculptures of Michelangelo are
so different one from the other. Each represents not only a thing and
its beauty, but also a kind of thing and its kind of beauty. There is the
beauty of broken yet eternal love in the *Pieta*, the image of the mother of
the crucified Son at the moment of her bereavement. There is the beauty
of an agent of God, rendering the law in its firmness and indestructibil-
ity, in *Moses*. There is the beauty of another divine agent, chosen when
a boy to do an act so brave that it changed the world, his chief virtue at
that moment was calm obedience. This is apparent in the *David*. These
things were apparent to Michelangelo, apparent in a way that few of us
can see. He was moved by them to make an image so that the rest of us
could see better too. The work of art would not exist if something had
not moved the artist so powerfully.

If Michelangelo was moved by this beauty in its various aspects,
what moved those who made the American Revolution? Of course
many things, but they chose one of them at the moment of the official
act of Founding, a serious moment. They found this thing to be and
to be within those "Laws of Nature and of Nature's God." They found
it in the natural station of man. They found it in his right to be ruled
by no other man except by his consent. They found it in that combination of assertion and obedience that is proper to a being beneath God
and above the beasts. The right of each human being to consent to the
government over him is unmistakable in the Declaration; so, too, is
the subordination of each human being to laws not by man; so, too, is
the superiority of the divine to the human; so, too, is the sanction of
the divine and the natural for justice among humans. The Founders
wanted to recognize, and for all to recognize, the right and duty of
all who are human to occupy the human station. What moved in the
American Revolution moved to this purpose. Called by this purpose,
it moved with a mighty force.

Even after we name these three powerful things, we still do not have enough to make our statue, and also we do not have enough to make our country. The material, the artist, and the object supplying the motive in the artist are not enough by themselves. The *Pieta* is not just about motherhood in its essence, sublimated to heaven; it is also about Mary (and her son), a young woman of whom we have some physical description. The *David* is not just about the heroic boyhood chosen by God as his instrument; it is also about a boy named David who lived and of whom we have extensive physical descriptions. God, being omnipotent, might have chosen some pony (blessed with reason), or some old man, to kill some giant as David killed Goliath, and if He did that, an artist could sculpt that pony or that old man to show some of the qualities that David possessed. But the sculpture would not look like David; it would look like a pony or an old man. The apostles must have been devastated by the crucifixion, and an artist with sublime ability could depict that devastation with sublime result; but the statue would then look like a man, not Mary. Similarly in the United States, the Founders might have set up an executive branch with two presidents (some wanted this), given the states little power (some wanted this), or made the judges electable and changeable (some wanted this). The country does not have its shape as a recognizable thing until it has its *shape*. And once it takes its shape, it is hard to alter it. Once the *David* is sculpted, the marble that would be needed to make a pony or an old man has been destroyed. Once the Constitution begins to operate, it makes other possibilities more difficult or impossible.

· · · · ·

What is the parallel, in making up the United States of America, to the person of the maid Mary or the boy David who gives definition to the *Pieta* or the *David*? When we think of the United States, we think of so many things. It is a vast country with stunning coasts, staggering mountains, and limitless prairies. Its people come from every kind of background and show it in their appearance, and yet there is a coherence to them that makes it meaningful to speak of an American as an American. These details and every other detail large and small about the nation are part of its identity or being.

But when we think of the United States doing something specific, when we think of it acting as the unit it is, we think of its government. That government, the patterns by which it acts, and the offices occupied by those who act are established in the Constitution. The Constitution gives the nation its shape, and by doing this, it exercises a powerful influence constantly on all that we do. In an earlier chapter, we described the Speaker of the House, Nancy Pelosi, revealing so plainly her contempt for the Constitution. It was a serious moment, but it does not mean that the Constitution is gone. She would soon be making heroic or scandalous efforts, depending on how one thinks, to maneuver her health care bill through two houses of Congress and the executive branch, and this she did by the skin of her teeth and through many sleepless nights for her and thousands of others. It would have been easier for her to succeed without the separation of powers, without even representation.

No doubt she thought and thinks the bill a worthy and fine thing, and so one can see why she might resent the Constitution. One can see just as well why those who oppose her would resent the fact that the subsequent election could not suffice to overturn her work: under our Constitution it takes two elections or three to make a major change and make it stick. Even after the election, the courts are looking at the matter of the health care bill, and other elections are coming. If the Constitution persists, these activities will continue right on schedule, and they will do that even if some of us do not want it. The Constitution does not give any of us the power to do what we want, right now. The Constitution may be in danger, but it is not gone. Not yet.

The Constitution then gives the nation its shape and its ability to act. It or something like it, we have said, is required by the Declaration of Independence. Therefore this question of the relationship between the two documents is really a question of the meaning of the nation. If the two documents are necessary, and if they mean different things, then the nation is not an integrated but a divided thing, and it was from the beginning.

Joseph Ellis writes that the Constitution differs from the Declaration of Independence in valuing "social balance over personal liberation." Freedom, he means, must give way to the requirements of society. Our personal good must be sacrificed for the public good. The grand ideas of the Declaration must be compromised or abandoned in order to achieve balance in the society. The Founders ran up against hard necessity, it seems, and so they had to learn to do different things than the things they set out to do at the beginning.

Sure enough the situation had changed very much in the eleven years that passed between the Declaration in 1776 and the Constitutional Convention of 1787. In 1776 a band of unknown commoners had undertaken war on the mighty British Empire. They were hardly able to keep an army together for most of the conflict, and what army they had was mostly kicked about the battlefield as if for sport. When the Americans were not running away from the fight, they were starving, freezing, and bleeding out their winters in the snow, or else they were hightailing it home to safety, away from the army and the cause it defended. Yet somehow the band of commoners won. They found a way to stand in front of professional armies and trade blows. Finally they came to listen to the cry of General Washington that they were free men, and the enemy soldiers were only servants, and servants should be the ones to run.[5] And then the servants did run, and also they surrendered.

Then the great Washington, now covered in honor, astonished the world by laying down his sword and retiring rather than claiming the right of the conqueror to rule. He and his rabble achieved a glory in the cause of human freedom never seen before, shining brighter for its emergence from forlorn hope. Hardly any scene in history is more touching than the farewells said among the commanders of the Continental Army at Fraunces Tavern before they broke up their ranks. Washington toasted them: "With a heart full of love and gratitude I now take leave of you. I most devoutly wish that your latter days maybe as prosperous and happy as your former ones have been glorious and honorable."[6] Then they said good-bye. Grown men wept. Washington held each one in turn in his arms. They were heroes, never overcome except by their love for each other and their wonder at the victory they had won.

· · · · ·

After that the glory began to fade. The new nation sank into a muddle. Pledged to the contrary, states made their own wars, signed their own treaties, and violated those signed by the nation. They did not pay the taxes they had agreed to pay. They stiffed the faithful lenders who had stood by them in their darkest days. They expropriated the rich and victimized the poor; they flaunted each other's laws. The young nation that fought like a Titan to win its independence became infantile in the exercise of it. Aristocrats in Europe sniffed that they had known all along that common people could not manage their own affairs without the benefit of kings and nobles. And they kept their European armies hovering around the edges of the new nation, waiting to seize their bit of the continent. The splendor of the Revolution faded toward shame.

This was an emergency of a new kind, and it is plausible that new means, and perhaps new principles, would be required to meet it. Who could blame the Founders if they were to change their minds about the ideas behind government, given that the problem of government presented to them after the Revolution was different from the one presented before it? Who could blame them for writing the Constitution in a way that departed from the Declaration?

Yet James Madison, for one, denied that the Constitution takes any step away from the Declaration of Independence. Arguing that the Constitutional Convention did indeed have the power to write a constitution of the kind that it produced, he said that the authority comes from several places, but finally from the "transcendent and precious right of the people to 'abolish or alter their governments as to them shall seem most likely to effect their safety and happiness.'"[7] This is a quotation from the Declaration of Independence itself; it claims the direct authority of the Declaration to justify the work of the Constitutional Convention.

Moreover, Madison denied that the Constitution takes any step away from the purposes of the Declaration in the source of its authority or in the manner of its organization. It does, after all, follow precisely the major features of constitutionalism suggested in the Declaration: it is representative, its powers are separated, and it forms a government limited both as to scope and to methods of operating.

Madison wrote that the Constitution must be "strictly republican." Nothing else "would be reconcilable with the genius of the people of America; with the fundamental principles of the Revolution; or with that honorable determination which animates every votary of freedom, to rest all our political experiments on the capacity of mankind for self-government."[8]

Madison then defined that republican form. A republic is "a government in which the scheme of representation takes place."[9] It is "a government which derives all its powers directly or indirectly from the great body of the people, and is administered by persons holding their offices during pleasure for a limited period, or during good behavior."[10] He continued, "It is *essential* to such a government that it be derived from the great body of the society, not from an inconsiderable proportion or a favored class of it; otherwise a handful of tyrannical nobles, exercising their oppressions by a delegation of their powers, might aspire to the rank of republicans and claim for their government the honorable title of republic."[11]

In other words, representation is necessary, and people may be represented indirectly. Also terms of office must be limited, but they can be as long as life, so long as that depends on good behavior. And the people broadly must be represented. The scheme of representation cannot favor any specific class; there is to be no nobility among the Americans.

These are the essentials. If they are not present, one does not have republican government. It is "sufficient" if these essential provisions are all present, that is, if the persons administering it are "appointed, either directly or indirectly, by the people; and that they hold their appointments by either of the tenures just specified."[12]

Madison made this argument in *Federalist* 39, a document composed to advocate the ratification of the Constitution in the state of New York. With it he justified all those devices that give the Constitution its structure and make it seem to many modern historians "undemocratic"—indirect elections, longer terms, and the unequal representation of persons in the Senate. Does this prove that James Madison turned against the principles of the Declaration?

That does not seem plausible when one thinks who precisely this James Madison is. When Madison speaks of a "political experiment," he does not mean a thing happening in a sterile laboratory where quiet figures move calmly in white smocks. He means a thing involving war and costing lives. Madison was not a soldier in the American Revolution, but he was a politician on the side of Thomas Jefferson, a wanted man. He put his own labor into the composition of the Virginia Declaration of Rights, passed by the Virginia Convention less than a month before the Declaration of Independence. The Virginia Declaration is nearly as eloquent, and fully as treasonous in the eyes of the king, as the Declaration of Independence. So by the time he was writing the *Federalist* in 1788, Madison had already a long experience among the votaries of freedom in resting their "political experiments on the capacity of mankind for self-government."

· · · · ·

The Virginia Declaration of Rights is an interesting document for our purposes. It was passed by one of the most consequential legislative bodies in history, the Fifth Virginia Convention, which convened in Williamsburg on May 6, 1776. It was the fifth and final successor to the original Virginia Convention that met for the first time in August 1774. That Virginia Convention came into being when the royal governor dissolved the Virginia House of Burgesses, at which time the House retired to a tavern and resolved to continue its work. It quickly issued the first call for a congress of all the colonies. This congress, the Continental Congress, would eventually adopt the Declaration of Independence and the Articles of Confederation to form the American Union. The seed of that Union was therefore planted in the first Virginia Convention, which began with an expulsion from the state house and proceeded through a tavern toward the founding of the greatest of modern republics.

The seed that was planted in the First Virginia Convention sprouted in the Fifth. On May 15, forty-four days before the Declaration of Independence, it declared the Virginia colony independent of Great Britain. That same day it instructed its delegates to the Continental Congress to move for independence for the whole nation, which Richard Henry Lee did on behalf of Virginia on June 7. On June 12 the Virginia Convention adopted the Virginia Declaration of Rights, written mainly by George Mason, but also by a drafting committee that included James Madison. Thomas Jefferson observed the work from Philadelphia, where he was representing Virginia in the Continental Congress and would soon write the Declaration of Independence. He sent plentiful advice, including draft language, all of it consistent in all major respects with the product of the committee. The Virginia Declaration of Rights uses much of the same language, and carries the same meaning, as the Declaration of Independence. It begins, for example:

SECTION 1. That all men are by nature equally free and independent, and have certain inherent rights, of which, when they enter into a state of society, they cannot, by any compact, deprive or divest their posterity, namely, the enjoyment of life and liberty, with the means of acquiring and possessing property, and pursuing and obtaining happiness and safety.[13]

The Virginia Declaration is similar to another document too. Much of it reads like a constitution—indeed, like *the* Constitution. And it turns out that the committee working on the Virginia Declaration was also working on a constitution for the new state of Virginia. The Virginia Convention adopted this new Virginia Constitution on June 29, seventeen days after it adopted the Virginia Declaration of Rights. The same committee wrote both documents.

There is significant overlap between the text of the Virginia Declaration and the Virginia Constitution, and both overlap significantly with the Declaration of Independence and the Constitution of the United States. So if the latter two documents are "incompatible," the Virginia Convention instituted this incompatibility in two documents that are as close as hand and glove. And then two of the people responsible, if one counts Jefferson as a collaborator, went on to write the Declaration of Independence and the Constitution of the United States, all the while remaining the closest of political friends. And they managed, somehow, to make those two documents incompatible as well? Modern scholars ask us to believe this.

The Virginia Declaration of Rights makes explicit what the Declaration of Independence says implicitly about separation of powers:

SEC. 5. That the legislative and executive powers of the State should be separate and distinct from the judiciary; and, that the members of the two first may be restrained from oppression, by feeling and participating in the burdens of the people, they should, at fixed periods, be reduced to a private station, return into that body from which they were originally taken, and the vacancies be supplied by frequent, certain, and regular elections, in which all, or any part of the former members, to be again eligible, or ineligible, as the laws shall direct.[14]

This means that the government of Virginia is to be close to the people, true enough. But it also means that the whole government will not be under the immediate influence of the people at any time because the people must do different things to change the executive than they must do to change the legislature, and they may not do anything directly to change the judges. *Close* to the people, we see, is a relative term. This is the first American Declaration of Rights to be passed by a legislature, and because such documents are an American invention, it is the first simply. And in this document, as radical as any written, it is not imagined that the whole government should be under the immediate control of the people.

The Virginia Constitution begins with a section almost identical to the middle section of the Declaration of Independence. It seems curious to a modern reader, if he is accustomed to the Constitution of the United States, for this to be so. When the Constitution of the United States was written, the end of the War for Independence was four years in the past. When the Virginia Constitution was written, the war was just beginning. And so the Virginia Constitution begins with a series of charges against the king that justify the making of a new government for a former colony. These are arranged in twenty-one paragraphs, most of which are the same in substance, and most nearly identical in language, to their equivalents in the Declaration of Independence.

The Virginia Constitution was ratified less than three weeks after the Virginia Declaration and organized the legislative, executive, and judicial departments to be "separate and distinct." No person could be a member of both, except that county judges could enter either house of the legislature. The legislature would be bicameral. The lower house would represent counties, cities, and boroughs, and the upper house districts that were larger and made up of groups of counties. Members of the upper house would have longer terms, and they would be staggered. Both houses would indirectly elect the executive, or governor. Both houses would also indirectly elect a Privy Council, or Council of State. Both houses would indirectly elect judges. Jefferson, by the by, submitted his own draft of a constitution during this process. His draft had substantially the same features, except the property requirement to vote was rescinded, and the separation of powers and the strength of the upper chamber were fortified.

In other words, the Virginia Constitution, written at the time of the Declaration of Independence, with the collaboration of the author of the Declaration and of the Father of the Constitution, employs the same kinds of devices of indirect election, extended terms, and separation of powers that restrain the ability of the people to have direct and immediate control over the government. If Joseph Ellis is correct that the Declaration of Independence and the Constitution of the United States are incompatible, then so are the Virginia Declaration of Rights and the Virginia Constitution. But this means that those two documents are incompatible with themselves because they are essentially the same document.

Section XV of the Virginia Declaration contains not so much a declaration of the rights of the people as an admonition about what is required, in them, to secure those rights. It reads: "That no free government, or the blessings of Liberty, can be preserved to any people, but by a firm adherence to justice, moderation, temperance, frugality, and virtue, and by a frequent recurrence to fundamental principles."[15]

To produce and preserve this condition, we shall see, is one of the prime purposes of constitutional rule. To do this requires considering something more about the people than merely their will. And it is in considering this additional thing that the need for these devices of limited government arises.

Another person close to the Declaration of Independence also wrote a constitution. John Adams, one of the prime movers of the Declaration, was not present at the Constitutional Convention in 1787 because he was on the business of his country in Europe. But between 1776 and 1787 he wrote the first constitution to be written by representatives of a free people and then ratified by popular vote.

The Massachusetts Constitution was ratified four years after the Declaration of Independence, in 1780. The people of Massachusetts had turned down an earlier draft constitution, written by the state legislature, on the ground that they did not get to appoint its authors. Fearful of "legislative encroachments," the people of Massachusetts called for a special convention in which delegates would be elected for the sole purpose of drafting a constitution.[16] These delegates in turn elected a committee of three from among their number. John Adams, who wrote most of the document and gave it its genius, led this committee. It is a work of beauty and inspiration. Like the Virginia Declaration of Rights and the Virginia Constitution, it fulfills in one place for the people of one state the purposes that the Declaration of Independence and the Constitution of the United States fulfill together for the American people.

As in Virginia, the Massachusetts Constitution begins with a statement of principle that echoes the Declaration:

> The end of the institution, maintenance, and administration of government, is to secure the existence of the body politic, to protect it, and to furnish the individuals who compose it with the power of enjoying in safety and tranquility their natural rights, and the blessings of life: and whenever these great objects are not obtained, the people have a right to alter the government, and to take measures necessary for their safety, prosperity and happiness.[17]

Article 1 continues:

> All men are born free and equal, and have certain natural, essential, and unalienable rights; among which may be reckoned the right of enjoying and defending their lives and liberties; that of acquiring, possessing, and protecting property; in fine, that of seeking and obtaining their safety and happiness.[18]

These are the themes, and almost the words, of the opening of the Declaration of Independence and also of the Virginia Declaration of Rights. And as with the Constitution of the United States and the Virginia Constitution, the Massachusetts Constitution proceeds to separate the powers of government; to build a bicameral legislature; to elect one branch from one kind of district, and another from another; and to increase the terms of office of the upper house to a longer duration. The judges are independent of the popular branches, and they serve during good behavior, which makes them independent also of the immediate opinions of the people themselves.

The Massachusetts Constitution, like the Virginia Constitution and the Constitution of the United States, uses elaborate devices to qualify the direct control of the people on the government. And yet precisely like the Virginia Declaration of Rights that precedes the Virginia Constitution, and precisely like the Declaration of Independence that precedes the Constitution of the United States, it names as its bedrock principle the equality of all human beings and their irreducible right to consent to the government under which they live.

* * * * *

Now we have three constitutions before us. One was made in Williamsburg for the people of Virginia. One was made in Boston for the people of Massachusetts. One was made in Philadelphia for the people of the United States. They all contain the same kinds of indirect, divided, and even competing grants of power. They all say they are built on the authority of the people, but they all restrain, qualify, and moderate the ability of the people to use that power. They all describe a government that is representative, limited, and separated in powers. It does not, therefore, seem to be an accident that these constitutions are written in the way that they are.

Moreover, the Virginia Constitution is contemporaneous with the Declaration of Independence. It is signed by some of the same people who signed the Declaration. The Virginia Declaration of Rights, passed at the same time as the Virginia Constitution, contains the same doctrine of rights and consent of the governed as the Declaration of Independence. Somehow then these rights that are named so gloriously in the Declaration of Independence inspire the very authors of that document and their friends to make, at the same time, constitutions that feature the same major devices that are suggested in the Declaration and are the hallmark of all constitutions in the Founding era.

It is time to ask, therefore, why these devices are necessary. Is it because the people cannot be trusted and some other body or group must be given the power to control or restrict what they do? Or is it rather that the people can be trusted in certain ways and not in others?

The answer is there to be found, and it is not so very hard to find. There is a clue in that curious Section XV of the Virginia Declaration of Rights, which says that the people must possess and exercise certain qualities in order to preserve free government and the blessings of liberty. There is another clue in Article III of the Massachusetts Constitution, which says that the "happiness of a people" and the "preservation of civil government essentially depend upon piety, religion, and morality."[19] Those who cannot control themselves, these clues suggest, cannot control their government. But to control oneself means that one part of oneself must be in control of another part. Which part might that be?

John Adams wrote the Massachusetts Constitution three years after the Declaration of Independence, but he wrote something a few weeks before the Declaration that reveals his mind on this matter. It is called "Thoughts on Government." During the writing of this essay, he was working with all his heart to bring the Declaration of Independence to be. One might think, therefore, that at just this moment his chief thought would be about the principles of government. But the principles of government are not the only thing on the mind of Adams.

"Thoughts on Government" begins by saying that *forms* of government are important. Adams quotes (or slightly misquotes) a famous couplet of Alexander Pope: "[F]or forms of government let fools contest, / That which is best administered is best."[20] He then says of this couplet that Pope "flatters tyrants too much."[21] He means that tyrants could not, or could not easily, overcome some forms of government. Forms are powerful.

To know what form is best, Adams says that we must first study the purpose of government. He states that purpose twice, a little differently each time. First, he calls it happiness, which consists in "ease, comfort, security."[22] Then, based on certain higher authorities, he reformulates to say that happiness is virtue. This kind of happiness, he says, is higher than honor because honor is only a subset of it. Government, he says, must encourage virtue and also depends on it.

Adams argues, then, that republican, representative government, built on separation of powers, will be most likely to achieve happiness of the people, which includes their ease and comfort and their possession of virtue. And he writes, "The foundation of every government is some principle or passion in the minds of the people. The noblest principles and most generous affections in our nature then, have the fairest chance to support the noblest and most generous models of government."[23]

To Adams, the city is the soul writ large. He quotes both classic and modern authors in this essay; he quotes authorities from revealed religion and from philosophy. He finds agreement among them on certain fundamental points. One of them is that the *purpose* of politics is the well-being, the good of the people. At the same time, politics *depends on* the well-being, the good of the people. It is not easy to be a good citizen in a bad country; it is not easy to have a good country full of bad citizens. The relationship makes a circle. What happens in the soul happens in the city, and what happens in the city happens in the soul.

This word *virtue* makes another circle. It comes from a classical word, meaning in the Latin "manliness," "valor," or "worth." That Latin word for virtue comes then from another Latin word meaning "man." The word for worthiness in a man and the word for man come from the same place. It sounds as if it might be redundant to say that a man is a "virtuous" man. If a man is a man, then he has, at least in some sense, the virtue of the man in him.

There is an old argument to explain this circularity. If you use that older root meaning of the term *virtue*, Adams might be saying that happiness in a man involves being a man, perhaps being fully a man, or perhaps being a good or a worthy man. We have discussed that word *good* already; it is full of rich meaning for organizing constitutions. Here let it be said that happiness, according to a classical argument known to all of the Founders we are discussing here, involves being the right kind of man, the kind that is most like a man or most fully a man. It seems then that a good political system would depend on, and also help to produce, goodness in its citizens.

We begin to form a picture now of certain grand requirements for constitutionalism. These requirements aim just as high as the purposes of government stated in the Declaration of Independence. These purposes are stated twice, first "to secure these rights," meaning the unalienable rights with which we are endowed by our Creator. They are stated second to be "safety and happiness." Rights (including all freedoms proper to man), safety, and happiness are the goods for which government aims. These goods depend on our practice of certain virtues. They depend therefore on the best things in us, and they depend on those best things being in control. In a government based on the will of the people, they depend on those qualities existing in all or in the great majority of the people, and they depend on those qualities being in control in all of the people or in the great majority of them. But we know that these qualities are not always in control, certainly not in all of us or in any of us all the time.

It stands to reason that no government can secure these elevated goods for any sustained period unless it is contrived in some excellent way. Very few governments in history have provided them for a sustained period. Moreover, no government, before the American government, had been based purely on the consent of the governed. To institute a constitution on this basis and to achieve these ends is a formidable task, an occasion of high hope and vast portent for the whole of mankind. Aware of this, Hamilton writes in the first *Federalist*:

> It has been frequently remarked that it seems to have been reserved to the people of this country, by their conduct and example, to decide the important question, whether societies of men are really capable or not of establishing good government from reflection and choice, or whether they are forever destined to depend for their political constitutions on accident and force.[24]

If we conceive the Founding of America as an artful act, then it stands to reason that it must have the attributes of artistic achievement. If we conceive it as a successful work of art, then its attributes of matter and form must be consonant with the purpose that calls forth the skill of the artist, and of course that skill must be advanced. Moreover, each component of success must be capable of contributing what it must for the work to be complete. We would not look then to the Constitution to contribute what was contributed by the Declaration. It has its own work.

The challenge of constitutionalism is to provide a form of government that will sustain effort in the direction of the proper end of government. It is not enough to proclaim the principles of government, even if those principles are inspiring and their proclamation vital. The *Federalist* begins with the assertion that popular government is nothing short of vital and also that it has never been fully accomplished. Here, he says, in this new nation, all the causes have come together to make an opportunity never seen before. Now at last the capacity of mankind to self-government can be vindicated. It would require a document of special quality to make that vindication.

This, argue the Framers of that document, is the quality of the Constitution of the United States. Let us see what they argue is special about it.

~ EIGHT ~

THE SOUL WRIT LARGE

WE LEARN FROM THE DECLARATION THAT THE PURPOSES of government are the protections of our rights, our safety, and our happiness. We learn from John Adams, and from the Virginia Declaration of Rights, that these goods depend on certain qualities in us that can be trusted with power and on the ascendance of those qualities as we exercise power. The qualities are not, however, by any means ubiquitous among human beings. In fact James Madison made his own preparation for writing the Constitution with a reflection not only on virtue, but also on vice. It is this problem of vice, and the requirement that government act in response to virtue, that provides the fundamental necessity of constitutional rule.

In April 1787, less than a month before the opening of the Constitutional Convention, James Madison wrote an essay calling for a change in government titled "Vices of the Political System of the United States."[1] In it, he lists twelve vices. They are the reasons the nation might fail, the reasons it requires a new form of government. The cure for these vices, Madison conceives, is the Constitution of the United States. It is the virtue necessary to heal the body politic.

One of these vices, Madison says, is found "in the people themselves," and it is "more fatal" (if that can be) than the others.[2] This vice begins where vices do begin: in the passions and the interests of people. It becomes a political problem when a person or a group of people pursue his or their passions or interests at the expense of the rights of other people or of the minority. It becomes the most severe political problem when the people animated by it constitute a majority because in a republican government the majority speaks for the nation, and it may do what it pleases.

Madison has a way of saying things that seems cynical at first, but not so much after one thinks about them. He says in this essay that the members of a dangerous faction have a motive to restrain themselves by "a prudent regard to their own good as involved in the general and permanent good of the Community." This consideration, he says, is "of decisive weight in itself," and yet it goes unheeded. Both nations and individuals forget that "honesty is the best policy."[3]

This is a commentary on the nature of people in two ways. In one way, they are forgetful of the rights of others, of their own larger interest, and even of the fact that "honesty is the best policy." In another way, the fact about people is that "their own good is involved in the general and permanent good of the Community," and this is of "decisive weight." We may harm the public good by the pursuit of our own interest, but we harm our own interest at the same time. We may forget it, but honesty is the best policy anyway. This lays a basis in reality for a reconciliation of the private and the public interest. This is an opportunity, not easy to seize, but there for the seizing. Human nature is revealed in the fact that the public and the private interest can be reconciled; human nature is revealed in the fact that people often do not see or do this.

The intractable problem of human nature gives rise to a set of intractable political problems. These problems are present in every political society, but they take a republican form in a republican society. For Madison, they are the "diseases most incident to republican government." Madison and his colleagues at the Constitutional Convention sought to devise for them a "republican remedy."[4] Republicanism, the principle of representation of the great body of the people in the government, is taken to an unprecedented extent in the American Constitution. Madison emphasizes this fact in *Federalist* 63: "The true distinction" between the American governments and others, he writes, lies in the "total exclusion of the people in their collective capacity" from any share in the administration of the government.[5] This is to be the first purely representative government in history.

Madison elaborated the same themes seven months later in one of his most famous essays, *Federalist* 10. There we learn that faction is the political manifestation of our passions and our interests. These become political vices when they animate us to act adversely to the rights of others or to "the permanent and aggregate interests of the community."[6] Our passions and interests cannot be expunged: they grow in our self-love, and they grow in the differences in our faculties, which are our natural property, and which give rise to differences in the material and other property that we hold. We have a right to this kind of property, too, but it divides us. It is the most durable source of the division among us. In a free system, these differences will thrive and grow. We will never give to everyone a uniformity of interests. Moreover, our reason is fallible and connected to our self-love: we cannot expect people to simply think their way out of the practice of these vices, at least not unaided. "The latent causes of faction are sown in the nature of man."[7] This means, logically, that it can infect the majority as well as it can infect an individual. For one thing, "important acts of legislation" are "so many judicial determinations . . . concerning the rights of large bodies of citizens."[8] In that case, the majority may be judging its own cause. Injustice follows.

Some have taken this to be a gloomy view of human nature, and in some ways it is. But the gloominess is not unrelieved:

As there is a degree of depravity in mankind which requires a certain degree of circumspection and distrust, so there are other qualities in human nature which justify a certain portion of esteem and confidence. Republican government presupposes the existence of these qualities in a higher degree than any other form.[9]

The new "republican government" under the Constitution will depend on these qualities of men that justify confidence, but it will not forget the other part of human nature. To find a way to distinguish them, and to rely on the one and not the other, is the difficulty.

We could get rid of faction by suppressing it, that is, by the suppression of freedom. "Liberty is to faction as air is to fire." But this, says Madison, is a cure "worse than the disease"; the cure would kill the patient.[10] Madison is willing to risk fire for the sake of breathing, and he is willing to risk faction for the sake of freedom. But what if one could have breathing and still keep fire under control, and freedom and still keep faction under control? How would that be done? It cannot be done, we learn elsewhere, by subjecting the majority, meaning effectively the whole society, to some will outside itself.[11] Madison does not like kings or privileged classes. He takes pride in the fact that there are to be no titles of nobility permitted under the Constitution. Aristocrats have passions and interests, just like everyone else.

. . . . .

Madison begins to offer the solution to these problems in *Federalist* 10. They have to do with the advantages of republican, meaning representative, government. These advantages, it will emerge, involve both external and internal controls on the government.[12] External controls have to do with the relation of the citizens to the government; internal controls have to do with the arrangements inside the government. These have powerful effects on each other, and they overlap.

Federalist 10 concerns two of the main controls, both external. The first is that representative government passes the public will through a chosen body of citizens " . . . whose wisdom may best discern the true interest of their country and whose patriotism and love of justice will be least likely to sacrifice it to temporary or partial considerations." This will "refine and enlarge the public views."[13]

This solution is helpful but insufficient. Representation does not always produce good results or good officials: especially in a small republic, "men of factious tempers" may "by intrigue" be elected to betray the interest of the people. Also there are limits to the capacities of most statesmen, even when they are well meaning. "Enlightened statesmen" might be able to "adjust these clashing interests and render them all subservient to the public good." Yet such statesmen "will not always be at the helm."[14]

To help cure the vice of faction, representation brings a second advantage. It is a very American advantage because it is specifically adapted to the situation and character of the American people. Americans have two habits that do not fit perfectly together. They give their trust to the government nearest them, the government most completely in their own hands. They like the local, the thing they can manage and control with the people they know. This follows from our sense of equality: we want to do it ourselves because we think we ought and we think we can.

Americans also have a habit, ingrained just as deeply, that is contrary to the first. They imagine their country the greatest in the world, and so they think grandly. The first legislative body to represent all the colonies called itself the "Continental Congress." At that moment no one knew for sure how big the continent was, nor would they have an official report of its size until the return of Lewis and Clark in 1806, a full generation later. The raggedy army under the authority of the Continental Congress came to be called the "Continental Army," which risked absurdity. But George Washington did not think it absurd, and he would eventually prove that it was not. Jefferson, like many of the Founders, would speak of America as the Empire of

Liberty.[15] The first *Federalist* paper thinks the people of this country will decide, "by their conduct and example," "whether societies of men are really capable or not of establishing good government from reflection and choice."[16] This mission for the country is like the principles of the country: it encompasses all mankind.

Representation makes it possible to capitalize on both inclinations in the American soul.[17] The country can be large and small. It can have, through representation, a government to encompass all the states and all the states that may be added; at the same time it can have a government for each state, separate and unto itself. The bigness of the Union will help to control the vice of faction. Madison thinks those wrong who believe that the small and the local can best stop the vice of faction by themselves: they make it worse. In a larger republic, each representative is chosen by a greater number of citizens, which makes it harder for vicious politicians to practice their arts. There will be a larger number of "parties and interests," and this will make it less likely that any one or any coherent group of them will gain a majority.[18]

This gives the impression, or anyway the impression is often taken, that for Madison the liberation of factiousness is the cure to faction. This is not true, but something related to it is true. The reasoning of *Federalist* 10 is in some ways parallel to the reasoning of Madison's contemporary, Adam Smith. The power of self-interest, including its power for good, is very great. As Adam Smith writes of the individual in a free market:

> He generally, indeed, neither intends to promote the public interest, nor knows how much he is promoting it. By preferring the support of domestic to that of foreign industry, he intends only his own security; and by directing that industry in such a manner as its produce may be of the greatest value, he intends only his own gain, and he is in this, as in many other cases, led by an invisible hand to promote an end which was no part of his intention. Nor is it always the worse for the society that it was no part of it. By

pursuing his own interest he frequently promotes that of the society more effectually than when he really intends to promote it. I have never known much good done by those who affected to trade for the public good. It is an affectation, indeed, not very common among merchants, and very few words need be employed in dissuading them from it.[19]

In political terms, the operation of self-interest helps to lay the basis for the kind of liberal society established in all the major laws following from the American Revolution. For there to be representative government, there must be an independent society to be represented. What happens in this society is private, not public, and yet it has profound public significance. If the interest of the butcher leads him to steal from his customer, there will often be war between them, or the law must intervene. If the butcher's interest, properly understood, is to give good service to his neighbor, and the neighbor's interest is to pay him, then there will be smaller need either for war or for the intervention of the law. The combined energies of people pursuing their interest in a lawful and private economy can work many wonders. When Madison writes that it is the "chief object" of government to protect the unequal faculties from which the differences in property arise, he is making a point not only about the private but also about the public good.

. . . . .

There is another advantage to bigness, and it cuts in a different direction. In a larger republic, Madison argues, communication becomes necessarily more open. It may be harder to keep secrets in a small place, but the one you want to talk with is always at hand: you can whisper to him. In a larger place one must speak more openly to reach the number of people necessary to make a significant force. Thus "where there is a consciousness of unjust or dishonorable purposes, communication is always checked by distrust in proportion to the number whose con-currence is necessary." It is harder to operate a conspiracy against the rights of others among a large group of conspirators. You never know who might be listening.[20]

The first advantage of bigness, then, is that it multiplies the num-ber of passions and interests. The second is that it helps to moderate and elevate them. Speech, to be effective across a large area and to a large number of people, must be fairer and truer than among a cabal. The justice of speaking candidly has a goodness of its own, and also now it appeals more to the interest of the speaker.

In America today we have television and the Internet, vehicles of instant mass communication unimagined previously. One might say that these prove Madison wrong. What do they show in the political debate except a clamor of distortion and cock-and-bull, self-serving and partisan? But does it not often happen that someone gets a camera and a microphone into a political meeting not meant for the whole public? And when that happens, one hears a tone that is very different. The per-son who yesterday was saying in a televised interview that he had great respect for his opponents and hoped to reach agreement with them says in private company that he hopes to push them in the ditch. Open communication must be more civil; it must appeal to a wider sense of justice. The effort to *seem* fair elevates the public debate and confines our speech to more reasonable points. Also it is harder to get away with pushing someone in the ditch if you have promised not to do it.

There is a glimmer here of what will become clearer. The right forms of government have a far-reaching and powerful effect. If running a conspiracy against the rights of others and the good of the community is less likely to succeed, the practice will not be so common. If speaking fairly and truly is more effective, those who can do it will advance, and at least some of those who cannot will practice the art. The right forms of government benefit the character of the citizens; good character in the citizens benefits the public good. It is another circle.

. . . . .

Representation makes possible another advantage concerning size. The government (and the nation) can be not only big; also the government can be small. It can defy political physics as they have been known: it can be large and small at the same time. Madison writes:

> It must be confessed that in this, as in most other cases, there is a mean, on both sides of which inconveniences will be found to lie. By enlarging too much the number of electors, you render the representatives too little acquainted with all their local circumstances and lesser interests; as by reducing it too much, you render him unduly attached to these, and too little fit to comprehend and pursue great and national objects. The federal Constitution forms a happy combination in this respect; the great and aggregate interests being referred to the national, the local and particular to the State legislatures.[21]

The powers of the states are said to work in "combination" with the powers of the federal government. Madison conceived them as a whole. At the Constitutional Convention, he and others argued for stronger authority for the federal government than it was given. He and his *Federalist* coauthor Hamilton opposed at first the compromise that gave the states control over the Senate. In the *Federalist* they began to make a virtue of necessity, and then to admire the virtue. At no point did Madison believe that either the states or the federal government was sovereign if sovereignty means the ultimate authority over the government. The people have that sovereignty. He had hoped that the people would delegate a larger share of the legal authority to rule to the federal government, but it was theirs to delegate, and that was not changed in principle by the Constitution, nor could it be. In *Federalist* 51 he writes:

In the compound Republic of America, the power surrendered by the people is first divided into two distinct governments, and then the portion allotted to each subdivided among distinct and separate departments. Hence a double security arises to the rights of the people. The different governments will control each other at the same time that each will be controlled by itself.[22]

Federalism, then, operates as a parallel to separation of powers. Like separation of powers, it provides an internal control on the government. It is the business of the states to check the power of the federal government, but also it is the business of the federal government to restrain the states. The Constitution presents the power of the states as the logical equivalent of separation of powers. There are seven articles in the Constitution, but only four of them concern the regular operations of the government.[23] The first three concern each of the branches of government. The fourth concerns the relations of the states to the federal government.

. . . . .

As with the external controls, so with the internal we find an arrangement that takes account of the interest and the passions of the people involved. We find an effort to enlist these interests and passions on the side of a good result. This result is defined independently of the interests and passions. It is a thing outside our wants, outside even our needs unless those needs are defined comprehensively.

These internal controls are necessary because the "exterior provisions are found to be inadequate." The "defect must be supplied, by so contriving the interior structure of the government as that its several constituent parts may, by their mutual relations, be the means of keeping each other in their proper places."[24]

The key to these internal controls is, therefore, in the separation of powers and in the division of power between the states and the federal government. Just as the external controls on the government are made possible by the representative nature of the government, so, too, is separation of powers. One cannot conceive of separation of powers in a simple democracy because the people are both the source of all authority in the government and the maker of the particular laws. When the people are assembled as a legislature and watching, no executive would dare to defy them. When they are away and distracted, the executive may run amok.[25] If, on the other hand, the sovereign is excluded from the operations of the government, it may delegate a portion of its authority to one place and to another, each then standing on an equal footing.[26]

According to the *Federalist*, it is not sufficient simply to write down the duties of each branch and assign different officers to manage them. These are mere "parchment barriers."[27] They will likely be overcome by the prestige and relatively undefined scope of the legislature. On this point Madison quotes with favor his friend Thomas Jefferson, who had written in his *Notes on the State of Virginia* a well-known passage:

> All the powers of government, legislative, executive, and judiciary, result to the legislative body. The concentrating these in the same hands is precisely the definition of despotic government. It will be no alleviation that these powers will be exercised by a plurality of hands, and not by a single one. One hundred and seventy-three despots would surely be as oppressive as one. Let those who doubt it turn their eyes on the republic of Venice. As little will it avail us that they are chosen by ourselves. An *elective despotism* was not the government we fought for; but one which should not only be founded on free principles, but in which the powers of government should be so divided and balanced among several bodies of magistracy as that no one could transcend their legal limits without being effectually checked and restrained by the others.[28]

"Not an elective despotism" might make a good subtitle for the *Federalist*. To avoid that fate, Madison writes that one must not only separate but also connect and blend the powers among the branches so as to give them "constitutional control" over each other.[29] In the Constitution the president has a share of the legislative power: he may veto bills. The Congress has a share of the executive power: it may oversee the executive departments and has control of their funding. The judiciary has a share of the legislative power: it may refuse to apply unconstitutional laws to the cases before it. The states have a control over the federal government: their legislatures elect the members of the Senate. The federal government has a control over the states: its Constitution is the "supreme law of the land," and its court rulings are binding on all lower courts.

· · · · ·

To maintain these controls inside the government, the Constitution once again harnesses the power of self-interest. Officials must defend their territory. Each department must have the "constitutional means" and the "personal motives" to resist encroachments from the others: "Ambition must be made to counteract ambition. The interest of the man must be connected with the constitutional rights of the place."[30] Madison is aware that he is not describing an elevated assemblage of the sages and the elders. He admits this in a famous and telling passage:

> It may be a reflection on human nature that such devices should be necessary to control the abuses of government. But what is government itself but the greatest of all reflections on human nature? If men were angels, no government would be necessary. If angels were to govern men, neither external nor internal controls on government would be necessary.[31]

This is another of Madison's seeming cynicisms, rising above cynicism. The existence of government proves that we are not angels and that angels do not govern us. The passage reminds one of the appearances of God in the Declaration of Independence. Here in the *Federalist*, as in the Declaration, the lesson is that all the powers of government may not be vested in the hands of a single being, except when those hands are the hands of God or His angels. Government exists to supply a defect that is inherent in our nature—we are not angels. This defect cannot be removed, only mitigated. It is apparent by comparison of the human with the divine. And when it is recognized, the distance between the human and the divine is diminished, if only a little.

Immediately after siding with Jefferson in *Federalist* 48, Madison takes issue with him in the next paper. He does this gently, amidst much praise. In a draft constitution that Jefferson prepared for Virginia, never adopted, Jefferson proposed a mechanism for two of the branches of the government to call, whenever they please, a convention elected by the people to alter the Constitution. This, Madison says, is "strictly consonant to the republican theory."[32] There is "great force" in Jefferson's reasoning, and Madison agrees that a means must be provided for a decision of the people on constitutional subjects "for certain great and extraordinary occasions."[33] But not often.

Not often because each appeal would "carry an implication of some defect in the government," and so frequent appeals would "deprive the government of that veneration which time bestows on everything." Governments "rest on opinion"; the opinions in individuals are stronger when they are widely shared.[34] "The reason of man, like man himself, is timid and cautious when left alone."[35] Then Madison writes:

A reverence for the laws would be sufficiently inculcated by the voice of an enlightened reason. But a nation of philosophers is as little to be expected as the philosophical race of kings wished for by Plato.[36] And in every other nation, the most rational government will not find it a superfluous advantage to have the prejudices of the community on its side.[37]

The Constitution, which is to be made by special process resting directly upon the people, will be their creature, but also it must have their veneration. This is important because neither statesmen nor citizens are likely to be philosophers. The arrangements in the Constitution are organized to couple power with restraint, power made more effective and consistent when restrained. Respect for this restraint must settle into the characters of the people. They make the Constitution, but then they must live within its discipline.

It is not only the people who must be restrained. The officers of government also have interests and passions. If these officers go to the people for a change in the Constitution, they will generally do so out of some interest or passion of their own. In that case the members of the legislature, more numerous and closer to the people, will have the advantage. But whatever branch is able to command a majority in altering the Constitution, it is likely to be animated by a partisan spirit inimical to the separation of powers. In such a case, Madison writes in a famous passage: "The *passions*, therefore, not the *reason*, of the public would sit in judgment. But it is the reason, alone, of the public, that ought to control and regulate the government. The passions ought to be controlled and regulated by the government."[38]

The classical description of the well-ordered soul is one in which the reason moderates and guides the passions toward good action.[39] Madison here is not calling for the elevation of one class of person over another. It is rather one capacity in the people that he wishes to promote. The city (or in this case the constitutional republic) is the soul writ large. If the reason of the public is guiding the government, then the rights of the minority and the "permanent and aggregate interests" of the community will be safe. This is the very definition of virtue, which we know from John Adams as much as from Aristotle to be the key to happiness. George Washington would give expression to this idea as well in his First Inaugural Address:

> [T]here is no truth more thoroughly established, than that there exists in the economy and course of nature, an indissoluble union between virtue and happiness, between duty and advantage, between the genuine maxims of an honest and magnanimous policy, and the solid rewards of public prosperity and felicity: Since we ought to be no less persuaded that the propitious smiles of Heaven, can never be expected on a nation that disregards the eternal rules of order and right, which Heaven itself has ordained: And since the preservation of the sacred fire of liberty, and the destiny of the Republican model of Government, are justly considered as deeply, perhaps as finally staked, on the experiment entrusted to the hands of the American people.[40]

This speech was pronounced by the chairman of the Constitutional Convention, who was also the symbol in our nation of the virtues of character. His comportment on the battlefield and his refusal to use the glory that he won there to demand political station won him that distinction. He was the man most qualified to deliver this pronouncement upon the purpose of the nation through its Constitution. It is fitting as well that the words were written by the man who must be the most competent presidential speechwriter in history, the Father of the Constitution, James Madison.[41]

. . . . .

It was a new step in the course of the American Revolution to build a Constitution that both represented and regulated individual citizens across the nation. It was a step that many were reluctant to take, and it was made only by compromise that preserved extensive legal authority in states. In this sense, those who say that the Constitution changes the course of the American Revolution are correct.

The American Revolution happened as every large human enterprise happens, one step after another. The Constitution did not spring full grown from the mind of James Madison the first time the British government made him angry. He and his colleagues worked and learned through war and struggle, debate and discussion. They got better at what they were doing. The Constitution of the United States is better than the first Virginia Constitution. Its structure is more elaborate, and it takes advantage of insight and of necessity in many places to make it so. The explanation of the Constitution in the *Federalist* is among the greatest modern writings about politics. These advantages were made possible in part by the fact that the Founders had already made their first attempts in Virginia and Massachusetts and elsewhere.

There was much disagreement at every stage of the American Revolution. Some were for independence and some for the Crown. Some were for a stronger and some for a weaker constitution. Yet the Constitution follows a pattern that is apparent in each of the major earlier steps that preceded it. It is more sophisticated as an instrument of government than any of those predecessors, but the sophistications are elaborations of that pattern. The Virginia and Massachusetts constitutions and the Constitution of the United States are things obviously of a kind, similar in form at a glance. Even inside the much shorter Declaration of Independence, a form of government is indicated. The protection of rights requires a government that is representative of the governed, its powers separated among branches, its scope and size limited to be consistent with a liberal and free society. Only such a society can be sufficiently independent of the government to hold the sovereignty upon which government is based.

The writing and ratification of the Constitution provided an occasion for a deepened understanding of constitutionalism. Politics, being itself a feature of human nature, is faced with all the contradictions that human nature presents. We are mortal beings with immortal souls. We live in a world of need, want, and partial understanding. We have at the same time the capacity to stand outside ourselves and judge our actions by a standard different from our needs and wants. Not philosophers, we have within us the faculty with which philosophy operates. The divisions and limits in these three constitutions are added for this reason. They are not added because the Founders wish to remove the government from popular control, but because they are determined to base it entirely upon popular control. This was at the time an unprecedented achievement in human history, still unsurpassed.

If the purpose of our lives is happiness, as the Founders agreed, then virtue is its substance and its cause. Virtue is not in ample supply. The virtue of the good citizen is not present in every citizen or in any citizen all the time. The virtue of the statesman, at its peak a thing of a very high order, is so rare that it appears in classic works as a synonym for *chance*. In the *Federalist*, these qualities are valued, and every device is deployed to encourage their presence. But their presence is not relied on alone. The best statesmen are too knowing to build a structure that depends too much on people like themselves; they build constitutions instead, and they hope for the right kind of ability to be available when it is needed. This kind of ability, too, is "much rarer than the largest and purest diamonds."[42]

Representative government places ultimate authority outside the government, which restrains both the government and the governed. In such a system, citizens have endless opportunity to talk, but they may act only on certain occasions. They are encouraged, therefore, to think, and to think together, before they act. The same restraints operate inside the government to encourage statesmen and citizens to the same habits.

Under the Constitution the institutions of government provide a better forum for good speech than for bad. They teach us to justify our actions before a court larger than ourselves, and therefore they teach us to look up to a standard that can be apprehended, and some little bit emulated, by our highest capacities alone. In teaching us that men are not angels, they tell us how we can attain a limited but beautiful quantum of this divine aspect. To attain it enough, and for long enough, to preserve our freedom and the goodness of our land is an achievement of constitutionalism.

Because the Constitution of the United States was written and explained by statesmen, and ratified by citizens in open debate, it is an achievement of the very statesmanship and citizenship that the Constitution hopes to sustain. In its structure, if not in its language, it shines with a beauty rivaling that of the Declaration of Independence, for it is an element and a condition of the same beauty. It is the soul writ large.

Conclusion

THE MOVEMENT THAT HAS GONE SO FAR TO ALTER OUR constitutional practices is now almost half as old as the Constitution. It has been powerful. Called from the beginning the "Progressive movement," it began in a combination of despair and hope, hope gaining intensity from despair.

The despair is evident in the doctrine of history. Woodrow Wilson wrote that "[t]he philosophy of any time is, as Hegel says, 'nothing but the spirit of that time expressed in abstract thought.'"[1] Of course this must apply to his thinking, too, which means that his thinking, too, was doomed to transience. He knew that. John Dewey wrote that the history of "liberalism is a history of phases," that the "conception of liberty is always relative to forces that at a given time and place are increasingly felt to be oppressive."[2] This means that his conception of liberty was transient too. Dewey knew that. Frank Goodnow wrote of the Declaration that "the actual rights which at the end of the eighteenth century were recognized were, however, as a matter of fact influenced in large measure by the social and economic conditions of the time when the recognition was made."[3] This means that the rights for which he contended were also a product of the condition of his time. He knew that.

Goodnow was a teacher. The first president of the American Political Science Association, he taught at Columbia, and he was president of Johns Hopkins. Of teaching, he wrote that those in charge of educational institutions are "under a very solemn obligation." On the other hand, he said,

> We teachers perhaps take ourselves too seriously at times. That I am willing to admit. We may not have nearly the influence which we think we have. Changes in economic conditions, for which we are in no way responsible, bring in their train, regardless of what we teach, changes in beliefs and opinions.[4]

A classroom is a very exciting place for one who has good students. Goodnow did. There is the magical process of learning together, of discovery, and from that process comes a bond that lasts a lifetime. In the classic works this experience is treated as one of the few highest things that human beings can do. That is because it can touch on the things that call us up toward places beyond time or condition. People give their lives for causes; in the classroom one may discover which of them are good.

College students are by definition unsure of what problems they will confront or what they will do when they confront them; they must study the rules that apply in all circumstances, at least if there are such rules. College, which derives from a word that means partnership, is ennobled by this task and also by the fact that it is done together, among friends, among human beings possessed of rational souls made by definition to talk at the same time they are made to reason. If nothing lasting happens in the classroom, it is denigrated. If whatever happens there can be overcome by "economic conditions," then the exploration "of beliefs and opinions" becomes less valuable. That is despair.

This despair also supplies the ground of a certain kind of hope. What about these "economic conditions"? What if one could manipulate them? Might he not then become the controller of beliefs and opinions? He would not be doing this by reason, true enough, and he would not be able to say that the beliefs and opinions that he produced had any standing outside the reasons for his manipulations. These reasons are located in his will, and the source of his will is in the pressures and economic conditions he has already encountered. It is a circle, one of a very different kind than the circle formed by the need for virtue in government and the ability of good government to foster virtue.

· · · · ·

History, then, is a story of circumstances playing on human beings. Human beings are shaped by these circumstances, and also they shape the circumstances back. We discover this through modern philosophy, a branch of science. Philosophy becomes a form of making. It supplies the hope that we can shape our world to fit our will.

The political hope of Progressivism is that science can be placed in control of administration. For this to be effective, administration must be unfettered. It must not be compromised or hampered in the way that separation of powers requires.[5] This will require a much larger government. It will require what Professor Klarman calls the new "fourth branch" of government, which is not restrained by representation or separation of powers. Still it will be a safe form of government. Safety would come from the high-mindedness of those who occupy the new places in government, from their scientific training, and from the fact that their interests would be taken care of (through good pay and long tenure). The Progressives attempt thereby to leave people like themselves in charge of the future, people who can be trusted because they are obedient to the creative canons of science. If the interests of these people are satisfied, then their interests will not be adverse to those of the rest of us.[6] To make assurance double sure, the new administration must be conceived as outside politics completely. On these conditions, scientific administration can take us to a society of greater plenty and closer equality than we have ever known.

These doctrines have, over the course of a century, transformed American political practice. The government now approaches half the size of the economy as a whole, and it may go where and do what it pleases. Our retirements, our health, and the relations inside our families are now the business of the federal government. Each business, large and small, is also under its purview. It is so pervasive that it seems to be the only way for the society to work. Moreover, the administrative state is now increasingly involved in the very electoral process by which the people exercise their sovereignty over political power. It acts as a regulator and as an interest group, its unions being one of the largest sources of funds for candidates and causes. The pollster Rasmussen has been doing a series of polls to see how many people think the government operates with the "consent of the governed." It has been falling steadily; in August of 2011 it reached a low of 17 percent.[7]

One last element of the contrast between these two kinds of government must be named: the new kind of government does not suffer under one restraint that guided and limited the original American government. It does not look to a sanction for its actions beyond the contrivances that we make, here among us in our time. Believing in a liberation of human power in order to do more good for human beings, it calls into question at the same time the whole idea of good. One may think it dangerous for this reason.

· · · · ·

Constitutionalism in the old sense seems a relic of a distant past. Article I, section 8, of the Constitution lists in seventeen paragraphs the things about which Congress may legislate. Half of them concern national defense. The rest mainly concern the guarantee of an unimpeded national system of commerce and property rights and the ability of the federal government to operate on the territory it possesses. There is no word about education, health, retirement, welfare, or any of the hundreds or perhaps thousands of areas of policy in which the Federal government now operates.

We cannot soon have a government that operates entirely within the confines of the Constitution. That will take a work of restoration and recovery of many years. It will entail the growth of civic institutions that match and surpass those built in early America. These must involve the whole citizen body in the job of running the government and the society. It will require that we take up again the hard work of approximating, so far as humanly possible, the principles of our land, which are so elevated that they can "never [be] perfectly attained."[8] It will require community organizing of a different kind. It will require that we abandon bureaucracy and centralized administration as a form of rule. The Founders thought that it was not mainly by dictating means but by sharing ends that free people cooperate.

Although it will take time to recover constitutional government, a start can be made now, and significant results can be achieved soon. We have to recover the meaning of certain principles, and we have to recover the methods of constitutional rule as they are exemplified by the best practices from our past. There we will find examples both local and national.

The central precepts of the American government are found in the Declaration of Independence, and they encompass the inseparable conceptions of nature, equality, rights, and consent. To know the purposes of the United States is to understand these terms.

Constitutional rule operates in service of these principles. Its genius is its ability to deploy but also restrain the use of power and to capitalize on voluntary action to advance the public good.[9] Observing America, Tocqueville remarks that he sees more government in America than he saw in France, which was the first centralized nation state. Of government, he writes,

In general, one can say that the little details of social orderliness that render life sweet and comfortable are neglected in America; but the essential guarantees to man in society exist there as much as everywhere else. Among the Americans, the force that the state administers is less well regulated, less enlightened, less skillful, but a hundred times greater than in Europe. There is no country in the world where, after all is said and done, men make as many efforts to create social well-being. I do not know a people who has succeeded in establishing schools as numerous and as efficacious; churches more in touch with the religious needs of the inhabitants; common highways better maintained.[10]

This is a picture of constitutionalism at work. In another place he remarks that a European obeys a public official because he represents a superior force, but an American obeys because he represents a right.[11] "One can therefore say that in America man never obeys man, but justice or law."[12] Tocqueville goes on to remark on the propensity of Americans to form associations and practice self-rule to the benefit of the society. To see government as the servant of the people breeds a certain energy and civic-mindedness in the people.

We have had welfare systems from colonial days, but they were organized locally and relied heavily on voluntary action.[13] Government itself meant something different because so much of it was carried out by the citizens acting as volunteers. Decentralized forms made possible, for example, the devotion of huge energies to education, which was always understood as the foundation of "an open field and a fair chance." The system of equal and decentralized property rights was seen as a great leveler. Not for America a feudal system in which powerful people have the say over the use of property by ordinary citizens.[14] The problems of welfare and education existed and were seen; the citizens found different ways to address them than we follow today.

In addition to examples of local and private action, we have in our past a rich legacy of national legislation intended to meet the same social problems that are now the province of the administrative state. These, too, were of a different character than we have now. Today we proceed by rules, detailed to the point of incomprehensibility, passed by administrative agencies that combine legislative, executive, and judicial powers in the same hands. Earlier laws met the key criteria laid down by James Madison in the *Federalist*:

> It will be of little avail to the people, that the laws are made by men of their own choice, if the laws be so voluminous that they cannot be read, or so incoherent that they cannot be understood; if they be repealed or revised before they are promulgated, or undergo such incessant changes that no man, who knows what the law is to-day, can guess what it will be to-morrow. Law is defined to be a rule of action; but how can that be a rule, which is little known, and less fixed?[15]

The Congress under the Articles of Confederation passed the largest single subsidy for education in American history. The legislators did this in the summer of 1787, while the Constitution was being written. The law they passed is the aforementioned Northwest Ordinance, which provides the method by which new territory can be admitted into our Union as free and equal states, not colonies. Together with its partner the Land Ordinance of 1785, the Northwest Ordinance provides for the immediate sale of the land in the Northwest Territory[16] into private hands to pay off the debt from the Revolutionary War. It reserves one section (1/36 of the whole) of each township to provide "education in that township." It states the purpose in Article III: "Religion, morality, and knowledge being necessary to good government and happiness of mankind, school and the means of education shall ever be encouraged." The gift of federal land was transferred as an endowment to the states, the federal government no longer to regulate. The Northwest Ordinance is just under 3,000 *words* long.

The Homestead Act transferred about 10 percent of the land area of the United States to unnamed private parties in lots of 160 acres each. The only condition was that a family live on the land and work it five years. Eventually more than 1.5 million people availed themselves of this opportunity. President Abraham Lincoln signed it into law in May 1862, and like so much that he did, it is among the most generous acts of government policy in human history. It applies to all. It can be read and understood by all. It is 1,380 *words* long.

These laws are shining examples of the grand constitutional practices of free government in operation. These violation of these practices is named in the Declaration of Independence as causes of rebellion against the king. They are reaffirmed in the contemporaneous Virginia Declaration of Rights and the Virginia Constitution, and in the Massachusetts Constitution that came a little later. They are taken to their highest state of perfection in the Constitution of the United States.

Such a government is representative in the source of its powers; therefore the opinions of the governed are constantly solicited and constantly refined; therefore the consent of the governed is constantly renewed.

Such a government is separated in its powers; therefore the governing and the governed are held constant to their purposes and improved both in deliberation and in action.

Such a government is limited in its scope; therefore the sovereignty of the people is preserved as a real and abiding fact. Such a government breeds freedom and responsibility by involving all in the work of governing.

· · · · ·

The genius of the United States of America may be found in the cooperation of all the causes that bring government into being. There is a set of principles that locate man in his place in nature, above the beasts and below God. There is a people, living upon a vast land, responding to the call of those principles to form the first self-governing nation in history. There were some statesmen, aware how unusual were their capacities, determined to use them for the rights of all. They wrote a Constitution that the people adopted to become the most enduring and successful in history. Because all these causes must cooperate to produce the freedom and justice that we have enjoyed for so long, all of them must be preserved or all of them will be lost.

Because the principles that our country serves, and the institutions by which it serves them, have a beauty hardly matched in all history, they sound a call that all can answer. In their attraction and in our response is the hope for a free people. That is the Founders' key.

PART II:
FOUNDATIONAL READINGS

The Declaration of Independence[1]

IN CONGRESS, JULY 4, 1776.

The unanimous Declaration of the thirteen united States of America,

When in the Course of human events, it becomes necessary for one people to dissolve the political bands which have connected them with another, and to assume among the powers of the earth, the separate and equal station to which the Laws of Nature and of Nature's God entitle them, a decent respect to the opinions of mankind requires that they should declare the causes which impel them to the separation.

We hold these truths to be self-evident, that all men are created equal, that they are endowed by their Creator with certain unalienable Rights, that among these are Life, Liberty and the pursuit of Happiness.—That to secure these rights, Governments are instituted among Men, deriving their just powers from the consent of the governed,—That whenever any Form of Government becomes destructive of these ends, it is the Right of the People to alter or to abolish it, and to institute new Government, laying its foundation on such principles and organizing its powers in such form, as to them shall seem most likely to effect their Safety and Happiness. Prudence, indeed, will dictate that Governments long established should not be changed for light and transient causes; and accordingly all experience hath shewn, that mankind are more disposed to suffer, while evils are sufferable, than to right themselves by abolishing the forms to which they are accustomed. But when a long train of abuses and usurpations, pursuing invariably the same Object evinces a design to reduce them under absolute Despotism, it is their right, it is their duty, to throw off such Government, and to provide new Guards for their future security.— Such has been the patient sufferance of these Colonies; and such is now the necessity which constrains them to alter their former Systems of Government. The history of the present King of Great Britain is a history of repeated injuries and usurpations, all having in direct object the establishment of an absolute Tyranny over these States. To prove this, let Facts be submitted to a candid world.

He has refused his Assent to Laws, the most wholesome and necessary for the public good.

He has forbidden his Governors to pass Laws of immediate and pressing importance, unless suspended in their operation till his Assent should be obtained; and when so suspended, he has utterly neglected to attend to them.

He has refused to pass other Laws for the accommodation of large districts of people, unless those people would relinquish the right of Representation in the Legislature, a right inestimable to them and formidable to tyrants only.

He has called together legislative bodies at places unusual, uncomfortable, and distant from the depository of their public Records, for the sole purpose of fatiguing them into compliance with his measures.

He has dissolved Representative Houses repeatedly, for opposing with manly firmness his invasions on the rights of the people.

He has refused for a long time, after such dissolutions, to cause others to be elected; whereby the Legislative powers, incapable of

Annihilation, have returned to the People at large for their exercise; the State remaining in the mean time exposed to all the dangers of invasion from without, and convulsions within.

He has endeavoured to prevent the population of these States; for that purpose obstructing the Laws for Naturalization of Foreigners; refusing to pass others to encourage their migrations hither, and raising the conditions of new Appropriations of Lands.

He has obstructed the Administration of Justice, by refusing his Assent to Laws for establishing Judiciary powers.

He has made Judges dependent on his Will alone, for the tenure of their offices, and the amount and payment of their salaries.

He has erected a multitude of New Offices, and sent hither swarms of Officers to harrass our people, and eat out their substance.

He has kept among us, in times of peace, Standing Armies without the Consent of our legislatures.

He has affected to render the Military independent of and superior to the Civil power.

He has combined with others to subject us to a jurisdiction foreign to our constitution, and unacknowledged by our laws; giving his Assent to their Acts of pretended Legislation:

For Quartering large bodies of armed troops among us:

For protecting them, by a mock Trial, from punishment for any Murders which they should commit on the Inhabitants of these States:

For cutting off our Trade with all parts of the world:

For imposing Taxes on us without our Consent:

For depriving us in many cases, of the benefits of Trial by Jury:

For transporting us beyond Seas to be tried for pretended offences:

For abolishing the free System of English Laws in a neighbouring Province, establishing therein an Arbitrary government, and enlarging its Boundaries so as to render it at once an example and fit instrument for introducing the same absolute rule into these Colonies:

For taking away our Charters, abolishing our most valuable Laws, and altering fundamentally the Forms of our Governments:

For suspending our own Legislatures, and declaring themselves invested with power to legislate for us in all cases whatsoever.

He has abdicated Government here, by declaring us out of his Protection and waging War against us.

He has plundered our seas, ravaged our Coasts, burnt our towns, and destroyed the lives of our people.

He is at this time transporting large Armies of foreign Mercenaries to compleat the works of death, desolation and tyranny, already begun with circumstances of Cruelty & perfidy scarcely paralleled in the most barbarous ages, and totally unworthy the Head of a civilized nation.

He has constrained our fellow Citizens taken Captive on the high Seas to bear Arms against their Country, to become the executioners of their friends and Brethren, or to fall themselves by their Hands.

He has excited domestic insurrections amongst us, and has endeavoured to bring on the inhabitants of our frontiers, the merciless Indian Savages, whose known rule of warfare, is an undistinguished destruction of all ages, sexes and conditions.

In every stage of these Oppressions We have Petitioned for Redress in the most humble terms: Our repeated Petitions have been answered only by repeated injury. A Prince whose character is thus marked by every act which may define a Tyrant, is unfit to be the ruler of a free people.

Nor have We been wanting in attentions to our British brethren. We have warned them from time to time of attempts by their legislature to extend an unwarrantable jurisdiction over us. We have reminded them of the circumstances of our emigration and settlement here. We have appealed to their native justice and magnanimity, and we have conjured them by the ties of our common kindred to disavow these usurpations, which, would inevitably interrupt our connections and correspondence. They too have been deaf to the voice of justice and of consanguinity. We must, therefore, acquiesce in the necessity, which denounces our Separation, and hold them, as we hold the rest of mankind, Enemies in War, in Peace Friends.

We, therefore, the Representatives of the united States of America, in General Congress, Assembled, appealing to the Supreme Judge of the world for the rectitude of our intentions, do, in the Name, and by Authority of the good People of these Colonies, solemnly publish and declare, That these United Colonies are, and of Right ought to be Free and Independent States; that they are Absolved from all Allegiance to the British Crown, and that all political connection between them and the State of Great Britain, is and ought to be totally dissolved; and that as Free and Independent States, they have full Power to levy War, conclude Peace, contract Alliances, establish Commerce, and to do all other Acts and Things which Independent States may of right do. And for the support of this Declaration, with a firm reliance on the protection of divine Providence, we mutually pledge to each other our Lives, our Fortunes and our sacred Honor.

[Georgia:]
Button Gwinnett
Lyman Hall
George Walton

[North Carolina:]
William Hooper
Joseph Hewes
John Penn

[South Carolina:]
Edward Rutledge
Thomas Heyward, Jr.
Thomas Lynch, Jr.
Arthur Middleton

[Maryland:]
Samuel Chase

William Paca
Thomas Stone
Charles Carroll of Carrollton

[Virginia:]
George Wythe
Richard Henry Lee
Thomas Jefferson
Benjamin Harrison
Thomas Nelson, Jr.
Francis Lightfoot Lee
Carter Braxton

[Pennsylvania:]
Robert Morris
Benjamin Rush
Benjamin Franklin
John Morton

George Clymer
James Smith
George Taylor
James Wilson
George Ross

[Delaware:]
Caesar Rodney
George Read
Thomas McKean

[New York:]
William Floyd
Philip Livingston
Francis Lewis
Lewis Morris

[New Jersey:]
Richard Stockton
John Witherspoon
Francis Hopkinson
John Hart
Abraham Clark

[New Hampshire:]
Josiah Bartlett
William Whipple
Matthew Thornton

[Massachusetts:]
John Hancock
Samuel Adams
John Adams
Robert Treat Paine
Elbridge Gerry

[Rhode Island:]
Stephen Hopkins
William Ellery

[Connecticut:]
Roger Sherman
Samuel Huntington
William Williams
Oliver Wolcott

The Constitution of the United States of America[1]

Note: We have italicized the portions of the Constitution that were later amended or suspended.

WE THE PEOPLE OF THE UNITED STATES, IN ORDER TO FORM a more perfect Union, establish Justice, insure domestic Tranquility, provide for the common defence, promote the general Welfare, and secure the Blessings of Liberty to ourselves and our Posterity, do ordain and establish this Constitution for the United States of America.

ARTICLE. I.

Section. 1. All legislative Powers herein granted shall be vested in a Congress of the United States, which shall consist of a Senate and House of Representatives.

Section. 2. The House of Representatives shall be composed of Members chosen every second Year by the People of the several

States, and the Electors in each State shall have the Qualifications requisite for Electors of the most numerous Branch of the State Legislature.

No Person shall be a Representative who shall not have attained to the Age of twenty five Years, and been seven Years a Citizen of the United States, and who shall not, when elected, be an Inhabitant of that State in which he shall be chosen.

Representatives and direct Taxes shall be apportioned among the several States which may be included within this Union, according to their respective Numbers, which shall be determined by adding to the whole Number of free Persons, including those bound to Service for a Term of Years, and excluding Indians not taxed, three fifths of all other Persons. The actual Enumeration shall be made within three Years after the first Meeting of the Congress of the United States, and within every subsequent Term of ten Years, in such Manner as they shall by Law direct. The Number of Representatives shall not exceed one for every thirty Thousand, but each State shall have at Least one Representative; and until such enumeration shall be made, the State of New Hampshire shall be entitled to chuse three, Massachusetts eight, Rhode-Island and Providence Plantations one, Connecticut five, New-York six, New Jersey four, Pennsylvania eight, Delaware one, Maryland six, Virginia ten, North Carolina five, South Carolina five, and Georgia three.

When vacancies happen in the Representation from any State, the Executive Authority thereof shall issue Writs of Election to fill such Vacancies.

The House of Representatives shall chuse their Speaker and other Officers; and shall have the sole Power of Impeachment.

Section. 3. The Senate of the United States shall be composed of two Senators from each State, *chosen by the Legislature thereof,* for six Years; and each Senator shall have one Vote.

Immediately after they shall be assembled in Consequence of the first Election, they shall be divided as equally as may be into three Classes. The Seats of the Senators of the first Class shall be vacated at the Expiration of the second Year, of the second Class at the Expiration of the fourth Year, and of the third Class at the Expiration of the sixth Year, so that one third may be chosen every second Year; *and if Vacancies happen by Resignation, or otherwise, during the Recess of the Legislature of any State, the Executive thereof may make temporary Appointments until the next Meeting of the Legislature, which shall then fill such Vacancies.*

No person shall be a Senator who shall not have attained to the Age of thirty Years, and been nine Years a Citizen of the United States, and who shall not, when elected, be an Inhabitant of that State for which he shall be chosen.

The Vice President of the United States shall be President of the Senate, but shall have no Vote, unless they be equally divided.

The Senate shall chuse their other Officers, and also a President pro tempore, in the Absence of the Vice President, or when he shall exercise the Office of President of the United States.

The Senate shall have the sole Power to try all Impeachments. When sitting for that Purpose, they shall be on Oath or Affirmation. When the President of the United States is tried, the Chief Justice shall preside: And no Person shall be convicted without the Concurrence of two thirds of the Members present.

Judgment in Cases of Impeachment shall not extend further than to removal from Office, and disqualification to hold and enjoy any Office of honor, Trust or Profit under the United States: but the Party convicted shall nevertheless be liable and subject to Indictment, Trial, Judgment and Punishment, according to Law.

Section. 4. The Times, Places and Manner of holding Elections for Senators and Representatives, shall be prescribed in each State by the Legislature thereof; but the Congress may at any time by Law make or alter such Regulations, except as to the Places of chusing Senators.

The Congress shall assemble at least once in every Year, and such Meeting shall be *on the first Monday in December* unless they shall by Law appoint a different Day.

Section. 5. Each House shall be the Judge of the Elections, Returns and Qualifications of its own Members, and a Majority of each shall constitute a Quorum to do Business; but a smaller number may adjourn from day to day, and may be authorized to compel the Attendance of absent Members, in such Manner, and under such Penalties as each House may provide.

Each House may determine the Rules of its Proceedings, punish its Members for disorderly Behaviour, and, with the Concurrence of two thirds, expel a Member.

Each House shall keep a Journal of its Proceedings, and from time to time publish the same, excepting such Parts as may in their Judgment require Secrecy; and the Yeas and Nays of the Members of either House on any question shall, at the Desire of one fifth of those Present, be entered on the Journal.

Neither House, during the Session of Congress, shall, without the Consent of the other, adjourn for more than three days, nor to any other Place than that in which the two Houses shall be sitting.

Section. 6. The Senators and Representatives shall receive a Compensation for their Services, to be ascertained by Law, and paid out of the Treasury of the United States. They shall in all Cases, except Treason, Felony and Breach of the Peace, be privileged from Arrest during their Attendance at the Session of their respective Houses, and in going to and returning from the same; and for any Speech or Debate in either House, they shall not be questioned in any other Place.

No Senator or Representative shall, during the Time for which he was elected, be appointed to any civil Office under the Authority of the United States, which shall have been created, or the Emoluments whereof shall have been encreased during such time; and no Person holding any Office under the United States, shall be a Member of either House during his Continuance in Office.

Section. 7. All bills for raising Revenue shall originate in the House of Representatives; but the Senate may propose or concur with Amendments as on other Bills.

Every Bill which shall have passed the House of Representatives and the Senate, shall, before it become a Law, be presented to the President of the United States: If he approve he shall sign it, but if not he shall return it, with his Objections to that House in which it shall have originated, who shall enter the Objections at large on their Journal, and proceed to reconsider it. If after such Reconsideration two thirds of that House shall agree to pass the Bill, it shall be sent, together with the Objections, to the other House, by which it shall likewise be reconsidered, and if approved by two thirds of that House, it shall become a Law. But in all such Cases the Votes of both Houses shall be determined by yeas and Nays, and the Names of the Persons voting for and against the Bill shall be entered on the Journal of each House respectively. If any Bill shall not be returned by the President within ten Days (Sundays excepted) after it shall have been presented to him, the Same shall be a Law, in like Manner as if he had signed it, unless the Congress by their Adjournment prevent its Return, in which Case it shall not be a Law.

Every Order, Resolution, or Vote to which the Concurrence of the Senate and House of Representatives may be necessary (except on a question of Adjournment) shall be presented to the President of the United States; and before the Same shall take Effect, shall be approved by him, or being disapproved by him, shall be repassed by two thirds of the Senate and House of Representatives, according to the Rules and Limitations prescribed in the Case of a Bill.

Section. 8. The Congress shall have Power To lay and collect Taxes, Duties, Imposts and Excises, to pay the Debts and provide for the common Defence and general Welfare of the United States; but all Duties, Imposts and Excises shall be uniform throughout the United States;

To borrow Money on the credit of the United States;

To regulate Commerce with foreign Nations, and among the several States, and with the Indian Tribes;

To establish an uniform Rule of Naturalization, and uniform Laws on the subject of Bankruptcies throughout the United States;

To coin Money, regulate the Value thereof, and of foreign Coin, and fix the Standard of Weights and Measures;

To provide for the Punishment of counterfeiting the Securities and current Coin of the United States;

To establish Post Offices and post Roads;

To promote the Progress of Science and useful Arts, by securing for limited Times to Authors and Inventors the exclusive Right to their respective Writings and Discoveries;

To constitute Tribunals inferior to the supreme Court;

To define and punish Piracies and Felonies committed on the high Seas, and Offenses against the Law of Nations;

To declare War, grant Letters of Marque and Reprisal, and make Rules concerning Captures on Land and Water;

To raise and support Armies, but no Appropriation of Money to that Use shall be for a longer Term than two Years;

To provide and maintain a Navy;

To make Rules for the Government and Regulation of the land and naval Forces;

To provide for calling forth the Militia to execute the Laws of the Union, suppress Insurrections and repel Invasions;

To provide for organizing, arming, and disciplining, the Militia, and for governing such Part of them as may be employed in the Service of the United States, reserving to the States respectively, the Appointment of the Officers, and the Authority of training the Militia according to the discipline prescribed by Congress;

To exercise exclusive Legislation in all Cases whatsoever, over such District (not exceeding ten Miles square) as may, by Cession of particular States, and the Acceptance of Congress, become the Seat of the Government of the United States, and to exercise like Authority over all Places purchased by the Consent of the Legislature of the State in which the Same shall be, for the Erection of Forts, Magazines, Arsenals, dock-Yards, and other needful Buildings;—And

To make all Laws which shall be necessary and proper for carrying into Execution the foregoing Powers, and all other Powers vested by this Constitution in the Government of the United States, or in any Department or Officer thereof.

Section. 9. The Migration or Importation of such Persons as any of the States now existing shall think proper to admit, shall not be prohibited by the Congress prior to the Year one thousand eight hundred and eight, but a Tax or duty may be imposed on such Importation, not exceeding ten dollars for each Person.

The Privilege of the Writ of Habeas Corpus shall not be suspended, unless when in Cases of Rebellion or Invasion the public Safety may require it.

No Bill of Attainder or ex post facto Law shall be passed.

No Capitation, or other direct, Tax shall be laid, *unless in Proportion to the Census or Enumeration herein before directed to be taken.*

No Tax or Duty shall be laid on Articles exported from any State.

No Preference shall be given by any Regulation of Commerce or Revenue to the Ports of one State over those of another; nor shall Vessels bound to, or from, one State, be obliged to enter, clear, or pay Duties in another.

No Money shall be drawn from the Treasury, but in Consequence of Appropriations made by Law; and a regular Statement and Account of the Receipts and Expenditures of all public Money shall be published from time to time.

No Title of Nobility shall be granted by the United States: And no Person holding any Office of Profit or Trust under them, shall, without the Consent of the Congress, accept of any present, Emolument, Office, or Title, of any kind whatever, from any King, Prince or foreign State.

Section. 10. No State shall enter into any Treaty, Alliance, or Confederation; grant Letters of Marque and Reprisal; coin Money; emit Bills of Credit; make any Thing but gold and silver Coin a Tender in Payment of Debts; pass any Bill of Attainder, ex post facto Law, or Law impairing the Obligation of Contracts, or grant any Title of Nobility.

No State shall, without the Consent of the Congress, lay any Imposts or Duties on Imports or Exports, except what may be absolutely necessary for executing its inspection Laws: and the net Produce of all Duties and Imposts, laid by any State on Imports or Exports, shall be for the Use of the Treasury of the United States; and all such Laws shall be subject to the Revision and Controul of the Congress.

No State shall, without the Consent of Congress, lay any duty of Tonnage, keep Troops, or Ships of War in time of Peace, enter into any Agreement or Compact with another State, or with a foreign Power, or engage in War, unless actually invaded, or in such imminent Danger as will not admit of delay.

ARTICLE. II.

Section. 1. The executive Power shall be vested in a President of the United States of America. He shall hold his Office during the Term of four Years, and, together with the Vice-President chosen for the same Term, be elected, as follows:

Each State shall appoint, in such Manner as the Legislature thereof may direct, a Number of Electors, equal to the whole Number of Senators and Representatives to which the State may be entitled in the Congress: but no Senator or Representative, or Person holding an Office of Trust or Profit under the United States, shall be appointed an Elector.

The Electors shall meet in their respective States, and vote by Ballot for two Persons, of whom one at least shall not be an Inhabitant of the same State with themselves. And they shall make a List of all the Persons voted for, and of the Number of Votes for each; which List they shall sign and certify, and transmit sealed to the Seat of the Government of the United States, directed to the President of the Senate. The President of the Senate shall, in the Presence of the Senate and House of Representatives, open all the Certificates, and the Votes shall then be counted. The Person having the greatest Number of Votes shall be the President, if such Number be a Majority of the whole Number of Electors appointed; and if there be more than one who have such Majority, and have an equal Number of Votes, then the House of Representatives shall immediately chuse by Ballot one of them for President; and if no Person have a Majority, then from the five highest on the List the said House shall in like Manner chuse the President. But in chusing the President, the Votes shall be taken by States, the Representation from each State having one Vote; a quorum for this Purpose shall consist of a Member or Members from two-thirds of the States, and a Majority of all the States shall be necessary to a Choice. In every Case, after the Choice of the President, the Person having the greatest Number of Votes of the Electors shall be the Vice President. But if there should remain two or more who have equal Votes, the Senate shall chuse from them by Ballot the Vice President.

The Congress may determine the Time of chusing the Electors, and the Day on which they shall give their Votes; which Day shall be the same throughout the United States.

No person except a natural born Citizen, or a Citizen of the United States, at the time of the Adoption of this Constitution, shall be eligible to the Office of President; neither shall any Person be eligible to that Office who shall not have attained to the Age of thirty-five Years, and been fourteen Years a Resident within the United States.

In Case of the Removal of the President from Office, or of his Death, Resignation, or Inability to discharge the Powers and Duties of the said Office, the Same shall devolve on the Vice President, and the Congress may by Law provide for the Case of Removal, Death, Resignation or Inability, both of the President and Vice President, declaring what Officer shall then act as President, and such Officer shall act accordingly, until the Disability be removed, or a President shall be elected.

The President shall, at stated Times, receive for his Services, a Compensation, which shall neither be increased nor diminished during the Period for which he shall have been elected, and he shall not receive within that Period any other Emolument from the United States, or any of them.

Before he enter on the Execution of his Office, he shall take the following Oath or Affirmation:—"I do solemnly swear (or affirm) that I will faithfully execute the Office of President of the United States, and will to the best of my Ability, preserve, protect and defend the Constitution of the United States."

Section. 2. The President shall be Commander in Chief of the Army and Navy of the United States, and of the Militia of the several States, when called into the actual Service of the United States; he may require the Opinion, in writing, of the principal Officer in each of the executive Departments, upon any subject relating to the Duties of their respective Offices, and he shall have Power to grant Reprieves and Pardons for Offenses against the United States, except in Cases of Impeachment.

He shall have Power, by and with the Advice and Consent of the Senate, to make Treaties, provided two thirds of the Senators present concur; and he shall nominate, and by and with the Advice and Consent of the Senate, shall appoint Ambassadors, other public Ministers and Consuls, Judges of the supreme Court, and all other Officers of the United States, whose Appointments are not herein otherwise provided for, and which shall be established by Law: but the Congress may by Law vest the Appointment of such inferior Officers, as they think proper, in the President alone, in the Courts of Law, or in the Heads of Departments.

The President shall have Power to fill up all Vacancies that may happen during the Recess of the Senate, by granting Commissions which shall expire at the End of their next Session.

Section. 3. He shall from time to time give to the Congress Information of the State of the Union, and recommend to their Consideration such Measures as he shall judge necessary and expedient; he may, on extraordinary Occasions, convene both Houses, or either of them, and in Case of Disagreement between them, with Respect to the Time of Adjournment, he may adjourn them to such Time as he shall think proper; he shall receive Ambassadors and other public Ministers; he shall take Care that the Laws be faithfully executed, and shall Commission all the Officers of the United States.

Section. 4. The President, Vice President and all civil Officers of the United States, shall be removed from Office on Impeachment for, and Conviction of, Treason, Bribery, or other high Crimes and Misdemeanors.

ARTICLE. III.

Section. 1. The judicial Power of the United States, shall be vested in one supreme Court, and in such inferior Courts as the Congress may from time to time ordain and establish. The Judges, both of the supreme and inferior Courts, shall hold their Offices during good Behaviour, and shall, at stated Times, receive for their Services a Compensation which shall not be diminished during their Continuance in Office.

Section. 2. The judicial Power shall extend to all Cases, in Law and Equity, arising under this Constitution, the Laws of the United States, and Treaties made, or which shall be made, under their Authority;—to all Cases affecting Ambassadors, other public Ministers and Consuls;—to all Cases of admiralty and maritime Jurisdiction;—to Controversies to which the United States shall be a Party;—to Controversies between two or more States;—*between a State and Citizens of another State;*—between Citizens of different States;—between Citizens of the same State claiming Lands under Grants of different States, *and between a State, or the Citizens thereof, and foreign States, Citizens or Subjects.*

In all Cases affecting Ambassadors, other public Ministers and Consuls, and those in which a State shall be Party, the supreme Court shall have original Jurisdiction. In all the other Cases before mentioned, the supreme Court shall have appellate Jurisdiction, both as to Law and Fact, with such Exceptions, and under such Regulations as the Congress shall make.

The Trial of all Crimes, except in Cases of Impeachment, shall be by Jury; and such Trial shall be held in the State where the said Crimes shall have been committed; but when not committed within any State, the Trial shall be at such Place or Places as the Congress may by Law have directed.

Section. 3. Treason against the United States, shall consist only in levying War against them, or in adhering to their Enemies, giving them Aid and Comfort. No Person shall be convicted of Treason unless on the Testimony of two Witnesses to the same overt Act, or on Confession in open Court.

The Congress shall have power to declare the Punishment of Treason, but no Attainder of Treason shall work Corruption of Blood, or Forfeiture except during the Life of the Person attainted.

Article. IV.

Section. 1. Full Faith and Credit shall be given in each State to the public Acts, Records, and judicial Proceedings of every other State. And the Congress may by general Laws prescribe the Manner in which such Acts, Records and Proceedings shall be proved, and the Effect thereof.

Section. 2. The Citizens of each State shall be entitled to all Privileges and Immunities of Citizens in the several States.

A Person charged in any State with Treason, Felony, or other Crime, who shall flee from Justice, and be found in another State, shall on demand of the executive Authority of the State from which he fled, be delivered up, to be removed to the State having Jurisdiction of the Crime.

No Person held to Service or Labour in one State, under the Laws thereof, escaping into another, shall, in Consequence of any Law or Regulation therein, be discharged from such Service or Labour, but shall be delivered up on Claim of the Party to whom such Service or Labour may be due.

Section. 3. New States may be admitted by the Congress into this Union; but no new State shall be formed or erected within the Jurisdiction of any other State; nor any State be formed by the Junction of two or more States, or parts of States, without the Consent of the Legislatures of the States concerned as well as of the Congress.

The Congress shall have Power to dispose of and make all needful Rules and Regulations respecting the Territory or other Property belonging to the United States; and nothing in this Constitution shall be so construed as to Prejudice any Claims of the United States, or of any particular State.

Section. 4. The United States shall guarantee to every State in this Union a Republican Form of Government, and shall protect each of them against Invasion; and on Application of the Legislature, or of the Executive (when the Legislature cannot be convened) against domestic Violence.

ARTICLE. V.

The Congress, whenever two thirds of both Houses shall deem it necessary, shall propose Amendments to this Constitution, or, on the Application of the Legislatures of two thirds of the several States, shall call a Convention for proposing Amendments, which, in either Case, shall be valid to all Intents and Purposes, as Part of this Constitution, when ratified by the Legislatures of three fourths of the several States, or by Conventions in three fourths thereof, as the one or the other Mode of Ratification may be proposed by the Congress; Provided that no Amendment which may be made prior to the Year One thousand eight hundred and eight shall in any Manner affect the first and fourth Clauses in the Ninth Section of the first Article; and that no State, without its Consent, shall be deprived of its equal Suffrage in the Senate.

ARTICLE. VI.

All Debts contracted and Engagements entered into, before the Adoption of this Constitution, shall be as valid against the United States under this Constitution, as under the Confederation.

This Constitution, and the Laws of the United States which shall be made in Pursuance thereof; and all Treaties made, or which shall be made, under the Authority of the United States, shall be the supreme Law of the Land; and the Judges in every State shall be bound thereby, any Thing in the Constitution or Laws of any State to the Contrary notwithstanding.

The Senators and Representatives before mentioned, and the Members of the several State Legislatures, and all executive and judicial Officers, both of the United States and of the several States, shall be bound by Oath or Affirmation, to support this Constitution; but no religious Test shall ever be required as a Qualification to any Office or public Trust under the United States.

ARTICLE. VII.

The Ratification of the Conventions of nine States, shall be sufficient for the Establishment of this Constitution between the States so ratifying the Same.

Done in Convention by the Unanimous Consent of the States present the Seventeenth Day of September in the Year of our Lord one thousand seven hundred and Eighty seven and of the Independence of the United States of America the Twelfth In Witness whereof We have hereunto subscribed our Names.

G°. Washington—
Presidt and deputy from Virginia

Delaware	Maryland
Geo: Read	James McHenry
Gunning Bedford jun	Dan of St Thos. Jenifer
John Dickinson	Danl. Carroll
Richard Bassett	
Jaco: Broom	

Virginia

John Blair—

James Madison Jr.

North Carolina

Wm. Blount

Richd. Dobbs Spaight

Hu Williamson

South Carolina

J. Rutledge

Charles Cotesworth

Pinckney

Charles Pinckney

Pierce Butler

Georgia

William Few

Abr Baldwin

New Hampshire

John Langdon

Nicholas Gilman

Massachusetts

Nathaniel Gorham

Rufus King

Connecticut

Wm. Saml. Johnson

Roger Sherman

New York

Alexander Hamilton

New Jersey

Wil: Livingston

David Brearley

Wm. Paterson

Jona: Dayton

Pennsylvania

B Franklin

Thomas Mifflin

Robt. Morris

Geo. Clymer

Thos. FitzSimons

Jared Ingersoll

James Wilson

Gouv Morris

Attest William Jackson

Secretary

AMENDMENTS TO THE CONSTITUTION OF
THE UNITED STATES OF AMERICA

The first ten amendments to the Constitution—the Bill of Rights—
were ratified effective December 15, 1791.

AMENDMENT I

Congress shall make no law respecting an establishment of religion,
or prohibiting the free exercise thereof; or abridging the freedom of
speech, or of the press; or the right of the people peaceably to assemble,
and to petition the Government for a redress of grievances.

AMENDMENT II

A well regulated Militia, being necessary to the security of a free State,
the right of the people to keep and bear Arms, shall not be infringed.

AMENDMENT III

No Soldier shall, in time of peace be quartered in any house, without
the consent of the Owner, nor in time of war, but in a manner to be
prescribed by law.

AMENDMENT IV

The right of the people to be secure in their persons, houses, papers,
and effects, against unreasonable searches and seizures, shall not be
violated, and no Warrants shall issue, but upon probable cause, supported by Oath or affirmation, and particularly describing the place to
be searched, and the persons or things to be seized.

AMENDMENT V

No person shall be held to answer for a capital, or otherwise infamous crime, unless on a presentment or indictment of a Grand Jury, except in cases arising in the land or naval forces, or in the Militia, when in actual service in time of War or public danger; nor shall any person be subject for the same offense to be twice put in jeopardy of life or limb; nor shall be compelled in any criminal case to be a witness against himself, nor be deprived of life, liberty, or property, without due process of law; nor shall private property be taken for public use, without just compensation.

AMENDMENT VI

In all criminal prosecutions, the accused shall enjoy the right to a speedy and public trial, by an impartial jury of the State and district wherein the crime shall have been committed, which district shall have been previously ascertained by law, and to be informed of the nature and cause of the accusation; to be confronted with the witnesses against him; to have compulsory process for obtaining witnesses in his favor, and to have the Assistance of Counsel for his defence.

AMENDMENT VII

In Suits at common law, where the value in controversy shall exceed twenty dollars, the right of trial by jury shall be preserved, and no fact tried by a jury, shall be otherwise re-examined in any Court of the United States, than according to the rules of the common law.

AMENDMENT VIII

Excessive bail shall not be required, nor excessive fines imposed, nor cruel and unusual punishments inflicted.

AMENDMENT IX

The enumeration in the Constitution, of certain rights, shall not be construed to deny or disparage others retained by the people.

AMENDMENT X

The powers not delegated to the United States by the Constitution, nor prohibited by it to the States, are reserved to the States respectively, or to the people.

AMENDMENT XI
Ratified February 7, 1795

The Judicial power of the United States shall not be construed to extend to any suit in law or equity, commenced or prosecuted against one of the United States by Citizens of another State, or by Citizens or Subjects of any Foreign State.

AMENDMENT XII
Ratified June 15, 1804

The Electors shall meet in their respective states, and vote by ballot for President and Vice-President, one of whom, at least, shall not be an inhabitant of the same state with themselves; they shall name in their ballots the person voted for as President, and in distinct ballots the person voted for as Vice-President, and they shall make distinct lists of all persons voted for as President, and of all persons voted for as Vice-President and of the number of votes for each, which lists they shall sign and certify, and transmit sealed to the seat of the government of the United States, directed to the President of the Senate;

The President of the Senate shall, in the presence of the Senate and House of Representatives, open all the certificates and the votes shall then be counted;

The person having the greatest Number of votes for President, shall be the President, if such number be a majority of the whole number of Electors appointed; and if no person have such majority, then from the persons having the highest numbers not exceeding three on the list of those voted for as President, the House of Representatives shall choose immediately, by ballot, the President. But in choosing the President, the votes shall be taken by states, the representation from each state having one vote; a quorum for this purpose shall consist of a member or members from two-thirds of the states, and a majority of all the states shall be necessary to a choice. And if the House of Representatives shall not choose a President whenever the right of choice shall devolve upon them, before the fourth day of March next following, then the Vice-President shall act as President, as in the case of the death or other constitutional disability of the President.

The person having the greatest number of votes as Vice-President, shall be the Vice-President, if such number be a majority of the whole number of Electors appointed, and if no person have a majority, then from the two highest numbers on the list, the Senate shall choose the Vice-President; a quorum for the purpose shall consist of two-thirds of the whole number of Senators, and a majority of the whole number shall be necessary to a choice. But no person constitutionally ineligible to the office of President shall be eligible to that of Vice-President of the United States.

AMENDMENT XIII
Ratified December 6, 1865

Section 1.Neither slavery nor involuntary servitude, except as a punishment for crime whereof the party shall have been duly convicted, shall exist within the United States, or any place subject to their jurisdiction.

Section 2. Congress shall have power to enforce this article by appropriate legislation.

AMENDMENT XIV
Ratified July 9, 1868

Section 1. All persons born or naturalized in the United States, and subject to the jurisdiction thereof, are citizens of the United States and of the State wherein they reside. No State shall make or enforce any law which shall abridge the privileges or immunities of citizens of the United States; nor shall any State deprive any person of life, liberty, or property, without due process of law; nor deny to any person within its jurisdiction the equal protection of the laws.

Section 2. Representatives shall be apportioned among the several States according to their respective numbers, counting the whole number of persons in each State, excluding Indians not taxed. But when the right to vote at any election for the choice of electors for President and Vice-President of the United States, Representatives in Congress, the Executive and Judicial officers of a State, or the members of the Legislature thereof, is denied to any of the male inhabitants of such State, being twenty-one years of age, and citizens of the United States, or in any way abridged, except for participation in rebellion, or other crime, the basis of representation therein shall be reduced in the proportion which the number of such male citizens shall bear to the whole number of male citizens twenty-one years of age in such State.

Section 3. No person shall be a Senator or Representative in Congress, or elector of President and Vice-President, or hold any office, civil or military, under the United States, or under any State, who, having previously taken an oath, as a member of Congress, or as an officer of the United States, or as a member of any State legislature, or as an executive or judicial officer of any State, to support the Constitution of the United States, shall have engaged in insurrection or rebellion against the same, or given aid or comfort to the enemies thereof. But Congress may by a vote of two-thirds of each House, remove such disability.

Section 4. The validity of the public debt of the United States, authorized by law, including debts incurred for payment of pensions and bounties for services in suppressing insurrection or rebellion, shall not be questioned. But neither the United States nor any State shall assume or pay any debt or obligation incurred in aid of insurrection or rebellion against the United States, or any claim for the loss or emancipation of any slave; but all such debts, obligations and claims shall be held illegal and void.

Section 5. The Congress shall have power to enforce, by appropriate legislation, the provisions of this article.

AMENDMENT XV
Ratified February 3, 1870

Section 1. The right of citizens of the United States to vote shall not be denied or abridged by the United States or by any State on account of race, color, or previous condition of servitude.

Section 2. The Congress shall have power to enforce this article by appropriate legislation.

AMENDMENT XVI
Ratified February 3, 1913

The Congress shall have power to lay and collect taxes on incomes, from whatever source derived, without apportionment among the several States, and without regard to any census or enumeration.

AMENDMENT XVII
Ratified April 8, 1913

The Senate of the United States shall be composed of two Senators from each State, elected by the people thereof, for six years; and each Senator shall have one vote. The electors in each State shall have the qualifications requisite for electors of the most numerous branch of the State legislatures.

When vacancies happen in the representation of any State in the Senate, the executive authority of such State shall issue writs of election to fill such vacancies: Provided, That the legislature of any State may empower the executive thereof to make temporary appointments until the people fill the vacancies by election as the legislature may direct.

This amendment shall not be so construed as to affect the election or term of any Senator chosen before it becomes valid as part of the Constitution.

Amendment XVIII
Ratified January 16, 1919

Section 1. After one year from the ratification of this article the manufacture, sale, or transportation of intoxicating liquors within, the importation thereof into, or the exportation thereof from the United States and all territory subject to the jurisdiction thereof for beverage purposes is hereby prohibited.

Section 2. The Congress and the several States shall have concurrent power to enforce this article by appropriate legislation.

Section 3. This article shall be inoperative unless it shall have been ratified as an amendment to the Constitution by the legislatures of the several States, as provided in the Constitution, within seven years from the date of the submission hereof to the States by the Congress.

Amendment XIX
Ratified August 18, 1920

The right of citizens of the United States to vote shall not be denied or abridged by the United States or by any State on account of sex.

Congress shall have power to enforce this article by appropriate legislation.

AMENDMENT XX
Ratified January 23, 1933

Section 1. The terms of the President and Vice President shall end at noon on the 20th day of January, and the terms of Senators and Representatives at noon on the 3d day of January, of the years in which such terms would have ended if this article had not been ratified; and the terms of their successors shall then begin.

Section 2. The Congress shall assemble at least once in every year, and such meeting shall begin at noon on the 3d day of January, unless they shall by law appoint a different day.

Section 3. If, at the time fixed for the beginning of the term of the President, the President elect shall have died, the Vice President elect shall become President. If a President shall not have been chosen before the time fixed for the beginning of his term, or if the President elect shall have failed to qualify, then the Vice President elect shall act as President until a President shall have qualified; and the Congress may by law provide for the case wherein neither a President elect nor a Vice President elect shall have qualified, declaring who shall then act as President, or the manner in which one who is to act shall be selected, and such person shall act accordingly until a President or Vice President shall have qualified.

Section 4. The Congress may by law provide for the case of the death of any of the persons from whom the House of Representatives may choose a President whenever the right of choice shall have devolved upon them, and for the case of the death of any of the persons from whom the Senate may choose a Vice President whenever the right of choice shall have devolved upon them.

Section 5. Sections 1 and 2 shall take effect on the 15th day of October following the ratification of this article.

Section 6. This article shall be inoperative unless it shall have been ratified as an amendment to the Constitution by the legislatures of three-fourths of the several States within seven years from the date of its submission.

Amendment XXI
Ratified December 5, 1933

Section 1. The eighteenth article of amendment to the Constitution of the United States is hereby repealed.

Section 2. The transportation or importation into any State, Territory, or possession of the United States for delivery or use therein of intoxicating liquors, in violation of the laws thereof, is hereby prohibited.

Section 3. The article shall be inoperative unless it shall have been ratified as an amendment to the Constitution by conventions in the several States, as provided in the Constitution, within seven years from the date of the submission hereof to the States by the Congress.

Amendment XXII
Ratified February 27, 1951

Section 1. No person shall be elected to the office of the President more than twice, and no person who has held the office of President, or acted as President, for more than two years of a term to which some other person was elected President shall be elected to the office of the President more than once. But this Article shall not apply to any person holding the office of President, when this Article was proposed by the Congress, and shall not prevent any person who may be holding the office of President, or acting as President, during the term within which this Article becomes operative from holding the office of President or acting as President during the remainder of such term.

Section 2. This article shall be inoperative unless it shall have been ratified as an amendment to the Constitution by the legislatures of three-fourths of the several States within seven years from the date of its submission to the States by the Congress.

AMENDMENT XXIII

Ratified March 29, 1961

Section 1. The District constituting the seat of Government of the United States shall appoint in such manner as the Congress may direct: A number of electors of President and Vice President equal to the whole number of Senators and Representatives in Congress to which the District would be entitled if it were a State, but in no event more than the least populous State; they shall be in addition to those appointed by the States, but they shall be considered, for the purposes of the election of President and Vice President, to be electors appointed by a State; and they shall meet in the District and perform such duties as provided by the twelfth article of amendment.

Section 2. The Congress shall have power to enforce this article by appropriate legislation.

AMENDMENT XXIV

Ratified January 23, 1964

Section 1. The right of citizens of the United States to vote in any primary or other election for President or Vice President, for electors for President or Vice President, or for Senator or Representative in Congress, shall not be denied or abridged by the United States or any State by reason of failure to pay any poll tax or other tax.

Section 2. The Congress shall have power to enforce this article by appropriate legislation.

AMENDMENT XXV

Ratified February 10, 1967

Section 1. In case of the removal of the President from office or of his death or resignation, the Vice President shall become President.

Section 2. Whenever there is a vacancy in the office of the Vice

President, the President shall nominate a Vice President who shall take office upon confirmation by a majority vote of both Houses of Congress.

Section 3. Whenever the President transmits to the President pro tempore of the Senate and the Speaker of the House of Representatives his written declaration that he is unable to discharge the powers and duties of his office, and until he transmits to them a written declaration to the contrary, such powers and duties shall be discharged by the Vice President as Acting President.

Section 4. Whenever the Vice President and a majority of either the principal officers of the executive departments or of such other body as Congress may by law provide, transmit to the President pro tempore of the Senate and the Speaker of the House of Representatives their written declaration that the President is unable to discharge the powers and duties of his office, the Vice President shall immediately assume the powers and duties of the office as Acting President.

Thereafter, when the President transmits to the President pro tempore of the Senate and the Speaker of the House of Representatives his written declaration that no inability exists, he shall resume the powers and duties of his office unless the Vice President and a majority of either the principal officers of the executive department or of such other body as Congress may by law provide, transmit within four days to the President pro tempore of the Senate and the Speaker of the House of Representatives their written declaration that the President is unable to discharge the powers and duties of his office. Thereupon Congress shall decide the issue, assembling within forty-eight hours for that purpose if not in session. If the Congress, within twenty-one days after receipt of the latter written declaration, or, if Congress is not in session, within twenty-one days after Congress is required to assemble, determines by two-thirds vote of both Houses that the President is unable to discharge the powers and duties of his office, the Vice President shall continue to discharge the same as Acting President; otherwise, the President shall resume the powers and duties of his office.

AMENDMENT XXVI
Ratified July 1, 1971

Section 1. The right of citizens of the United States, who are eighteen years of age or older, to vote shall not be denied or abridged by the United States or by any State on account of age.

Section 2. The Congress shall have power to enforce this article by appropriate legislation.

AMENDMENT XXVII
Ratified May 7, 1992

No law, varying the compensation for the services of the Senators and Representatives, shall take effect, until an election of Representatives shall have intervened.

Federalist No. 10: The Union as a Safeguard Against Domestic Faction and Insurrection (Continued)[1]

PUBLIUS (JAMES MADISON) * NOVEMBER 22, 1787

AMONG THE NUMEROUS ADVANTAGES PROMISED BY A well-constructed Union, none deserves to be more accurately developed than its tendency to break and control the violence of faction. The friend of popular governments never finds himself so much alarmed for their character and fate as when he contemplates their propensity to this dangerous vice. He will not fail, therefore, to set a due value on any plan which, without violating the principles to which he is attached, provides a proper cure for it. The instability, injustice, and confusion introduced into the public councils have, in truth, been the mortal diseases under which popular governments have everywhere perished, as they continue to be the favorite and fruitful topics from which the adversaries to liberty derive their most specious declamations. The valuable improvements made by the American constitutions on the popular models, both ancient and modern, cannot certainly be too much admired; but it would be an unwarrantable partiality to contend that they have as effectually obviated the danger on this side, as was wished and expected. Complaints are everywhere heard from our most considerate and virtuous citizens, equally the friends of public and private faith and of public and personal liberty, that our governments are too unstable, that the public good is disregarded in the conflicts of rival parties, and that measures are too often decided, not according to the rules of justice and the rights of the minor party, but by the superior force of an interested and overbearing majority. However anxiously we may wish that these complaints had no foundation, the evidence of known facts will not permit us to deny that they are in some degree true. It will be found, indeed, on a candid review of our situation, that some of the distresses under which we labor have been erroneously charged on the operation of our governments; but it will be found, at the same time, that other causes will not alone account for many of our heaviest misfortunes; and, particularly, for that prevailing and increasing distrust of public engagements and alarm for private rights which are echoed from one end of the continent to the other. These must be chiefly, if not wholly, effects of the unsteadiness and injustice with which a factious spirit has tainted our public administration.

By a faction I understand a number of citizens, whether amounting to a majority or minority of the whole, who are united and actuated by some common impulse of passion, or of interest, adverse to the rights of other citizens, or to the permanent and aggregate interests of the community.

There are two methods of curing the mischiefs of faction: the one, by removing its causes; the other, by controlling its effects.

There are again two methods of removing the causes of faction:

the one, by destroying the liberty which is essential to its existence; the other, by giving to every citizen the same opinions, the same passions, and the same interests.

It could never be more truly said than of the first remedy that it is worse than the disease. Liberty is to faction, what air is to fire, an aliment without which it instantly expires. But it could not be a lesser folly to abolish liberty, which is essential to political life, because it nourishes faction than it would be to wish the annihilation of air, which is essential to animal life, because it imparts to fire its destructive agency.

The second expedient is as impracticable as the first would be unwise. As long as the reason of man continues fallible, and he is at liberty to exercise it, different opinions will be formed. As long as the connection subsists between his reason and his self-love, his opinions and his passions will have a reciprocal influence on each other; and the former will be objects to which the latter will attach themselves. The diversity in the faculties of men, from which the rights of property originate, is not less an insuperable obstacle to a uniformity of interests. The protection of these faculties is the first object of government. From the protection of different and unequal faculties of acquiring property, the possession of different degrees and kinds of property immediately results; and from the influence of these on the sentiments and views of the respective proprietors ensues a division of the society into different interests and parties.

The latent causes of faction are thus sown in the nature of man; and we see them everywhere brought into different degrees of activity, according to the different circumstances of civil society. A zeal for different opinions concerning religion, concerning government and many other points, as well of speculation as of practice; an attachment to different leaders ambitiously contending for pre-eminence and power; or to persons of other descriptions whose fortunes have been interesting to the human passions, have, in turn, divided mankind into parties, inflamed them with mutual animosity, and rendered them much more disposed to vex and oppress each other, than to cooperate for their common good. So strong is this propensity of mankind to fall into mutual animosities that where no substantial occasion presents itself, the most frivolous and fanciful distinctions have been sufficient to kindle their unfriendly passions and excite their most violent conflicts. But the most common and durable source of factions has been the various and unequal distribution of property. Those who hold and those who are without property have ever formed distinct interests in society. Those who are creditors, and those who are debtors, fall under a like discrimination. A landed interest, a manufacturing interest, a mercantile interest, a moneyed interest, with many lesser interests, grow up of necessity in civilized nations, and divide them into different classes, actuated by different sentiments and views. The regulation of these various and interfering interests forms the principal task of modern legislation and involves the spirit of party and faction in the necessary and ordinary operations of government.

No man is allowed to be a judge in his own cause because his interest would certainly bias his judgment, and, not improbably, corrupt his integrity. With equal, nay with greater reason, a body of men are unfit to be both judges and parties at the same time; yet what are many of the most important acts of legislation but so many judicial determinations, not indeed concerning the rights of single persons, but concerning the rights of large bodies of citizens? And what are the different classes of legislators but advocates and parties to the causes which they determine? Is a law proposed concerning private debts? It is a question to which the creditors are parties on one side and the debtors on the other. Justice ought to hold the balance between them. Yet the parties are, and must be, themselves the judges; and the most numerous party, or, in other words, the most powerful faction must be expected to prevail. Shall domestic manufactures be encouraged, and in what degree, by restrictions on foreign manufactures? are questions which would be differently decided by the landed and the manufacturing classes; and probably by neither with a sole regard to justice and the public good. The apportionment of taxes on the various descriptions of property is an act which seems to require the most exact impartiality; yet there is, perhaps, no legislative act in which greater opportunity and temptation are given to a predominant party to trample on the rules of justice. Every shilling with which they over-burden the inferior number is a shilling saved to their own pockets.

It is in vain to say that enlightened statesmen will be able to adjust these clashing interests and render them all subservient to the public good. Enlightened statesmen will not always be at the helm. Nor, in many cases, can such an adjustment be made at all without taking into view indirect and remote considerations, which will rarely prevail over the immediate interest which one party may find in disregarding the rights of another or the good of the whole.

The inference to which we are brought is that the *causes* of faction cannot be removed; and that relief is only to be sought in the means of controlling its *effects*.

If a faction consists of less than a majority, relief is supplied by the republican principle, which enables the majority to defeat its sinister views by regular vote. It may clog the administration, it may convulse the society; but it will be unable to execute and mask its violence under the forms of the Constitution. When a majority is included in a fac-tion, the form of popular government, on the other hand, enables it to sacrifice to its ruling passion or interest both the public good and the rights of other citizens. To secure the public good and private rights against the danger of such a faction, and at the same time to preserve the spirit and the form of popular government, is then the great object to which our enquiries are directed. Let me add that it is the great desideratum by which alone this form of government can be rescued from the opprobrium under which it has so long labored and be rec-ommended to the esteem and adoption of mankind.

By what means is this object attainable? Evidently by one of two only. Either the existence of the same passion or interest in a majority at the same time must be prevented, or the majority, having such coex-istent passion or interest, must be rendered, by their number and local situation, unable to concert and carry into effect schemes of oppression. If the impulse and the opportunity be suffered to coincide, we well know that neither moral nor religious motives can be relied on as an adequate control. They are not found to be such on the injustice and violence of individuals, and lose their efficacy in proportion to the number combined together, that is, in proportion as their efficacy becomes needful.

From this view of the subject it may be concluded that a pure democracy, by which I mean a society consisting of a small number of citizens, who assemble and administer the government in person, can admit of no cure for the mischiefs of faction. A common passion or interest will, in almost every case, be felt by a majority of the whole; a communication and concert results from the form of government itself; and there is nothing to check the inducements to sacrifice the weaker party or an obnoxious individual. Hence it is that such democracies have ever been spectacles of turbulence and contention; have ever been found incompatible with personal security or the rights of property; and have in general been as short in their lives as they have been violent in their deaths. Theoretic politicians, who have patronized this species of government, have erroneously supposed that by reducing mankind to a perfect equality in their political rights, they would at the same time be perfectly equalized and assimilated in their possessions, their opinions, and their passions.

A republic, by which I mean a government in which the scheme of representation takes place, opens a different prospect and promises the cure for which we are seeking. Let us examine the points in which it varies from pure democracy, and we shall comprehend both the nature of the cure and the efficacy which it must derive from the Union.

The two great points of difference between a democracy and a republic are: first, the delegation of the government, in the latter, to a small number of citizens elected by the rest; secondly, the greater number of citizens and greater sphere of country over which the latter may be extended.

The effect of the first difference is, on the one hand, to refine and enlarge the public views by passing them through the medium of a chosen body of citizens, whose wisdom may best discern the true interest of their country and whose patriotism and love of justice will be least likely to sacrifice it to temporary or partial considerations. Under such a regulation, it may well happen that the public voice, pronounced by the representatives of the people, will be more consonant to the public good, than if pronounced by the people themselves, convened for the purpose. On the other hand, the effect may be inverted. Men of factious tempers, of local prejudices, or of sinister designs, may, by intrigue, by corruption, or by other means, first obtain the suffrages, and then betray the interests of the people. The question resulting is, whether small or extensive republics are most favorable to the election of proper guardians of the public weal; and it is clearly decided in favor of the latter by two obvious considerations.

In the first place it is to be remarked that however small the Republic may be, the Representatives must be raised to a certain number, in order to guard against the cabals of a few; and that however large it may be, they must be limited to a certain number, in order to guard against the confusion of a multitude. Hence, the number of representatives in the two cases not being in proportion to that of the constituents, and being proportionally greatest in the small republic, it follows that if the proportion of fit characters be not less in the large than in the small republic the former will present a greater option, and consequently a greater probability of a fit choice.

In the next place, as each representative will be chosen by a greater number of citizens in the large than in the small republic, it will be more difficult for unworthy candidates to practice with success the vicious arts by which elections are too often carried; and the suffrages of the people being more free, will be more likely to center on men who possess the most attractive merit and the most diffusive and established characters.

It must be confessed that in this, as in most other cases, there is a mean, on both sides of which inconveniences will be found to lie.

By enlarging too much the number of electors, you render the representative too little acquainted with all their local circumstances and lesser interests; as by reducing it too much, you render him unduly attached to these, and too little fit to comprehend and pursue great and national objects. The federal Constitution forms a happy combination in this respect; the great and aggregate interests being referred to the national, the local and particular to the State legislatures.

The other point of difference is the greater number of citizens and extent of territory which may be brought within the compass of republican than of democratic government; and it is this circumstance principally which renders factious combinations less to be dreaded in the former than in the latter. The smaller the society, the fewer probably will be the distinct parties and interests composing it; the fewer the distinct parties and interests, the more frequently will a majority be found of the same party; and the smaller the number of individuals composing a majority, and the smaller the compass within which they are placed, the more easily will they concert and execute their plans of oppression. Extend the sphere and you take in a greater variety of parties and interests; you make it less probable that a majority of the whole will have a common motive to invade the rights of other citizens; or if such a common motive exists, it will be more difficult for all who feel it to discover their own strength and to act in unison with each other. Besides other impediments, it may be remarked, that where there is a consciousness of unjust or dishonorable purposes, communication is always checked by distrust in proportion to the number whose concurrence is necessary.

Hence, it clearly appears that the same advantage which a republic has over a democracy in controlling the effects of faction is enjoyed by a large over a small republic,—is enjoyed by the Union over the States composing it. Does this advantage consist in the substitution of representatives whose enlightened views and virtuous sentiments render them superior to local prejudices and to schemes of injustice? It will not be denied that the representation of the Union will be most likely to possess these requisite endowments. Does it consist in the greater security afforded by a greater variety of parties, against the event of any one party being able to outnumber and oppress the rest? In an equal degree, does the increased variety of parties comprised within the Union increase this security? Does it, in fine, consist in the greater obstacles opposed to the concert and accomplishment of the secret wishes of an unjust and interested majority? Here again the extent of the Union gives it the most palpable advantage.

The influence of factious leaders may kindle a flame within their particular States but will be unable to spread a general conflagration through the other States. A religious sect may degenerate into a political faction in a part of the Confederacy; but the variety of sects dispersed over the entire face of it must secure the national councils against any danger from that source. A rage for paper money, for an abolition of debts, for an equal division of property, or for any other improper or wicked project, will be less apt to pervade the whole body of the Union than a particular member of it, in the same proportion as such a malady is more likely to taint a particular county or district than an entire State.

In the extent and proper structure of the Union, therefore, we behold a republican remedy for the diseases most incident to republican government. And according to the degree of pleasure and pride we feel in being republicans ought to be our zeal in cherishing the spirit and supporting the character of federalists.

PUBLIUS

Federalist No. 39: The Conformity of the Plan to Republican Principles[1]

PUBLIUS (JAMES MADISON) * JANUARY 16, 1788

THE LAST PAPER HAVING CONCLUDED THE OBSERVATIONS which were meant to introduce a candid survey of the plan of government reported by the convention, we now proceed to the execution of that part of our undertaking.

The first question that offers itself is whether the general form and aspect of the government be strictly republican. It is evident that no other form would be reconcilable with the genius of the people of America; with the fundamental principles of the Revolution; or with that honorable determination which animates every votary of freedom, to rest all our political experiments on the capacity of mankind for self-government. If the plan of the convention, therefore, be found to depart from the republican character, its advocates must abandon it as no longer defensible.

What, then, are the distinctive characters of the republican form?

Were an answer to this question to be sought, not by recurring to principles but in the application of the term by political writers to the constitution of different States, no satisfactory one would ever be found. Holland, in which no particle of the supreme authority is derived from the people, has passed almost universally under the denomination of a republic. The same title has been bestowed on Venice, where absolute power over the great body of the people is exercised in the most absolute manner by a small body of hereditary nobles. Poland, which is a mixture of aristocracy and of monarchy in their worst forms, has been dignified with the same appellation. The government of England, which has one republican branch only, combined with an hereditary aristocracy and monarchy, has with equal impropriety been frequently placed on the list of republics. These examples, which are nearly as dissimilar to each other as to a genuine republic, show the extreme inaccuracy with which the term has been used in political disquisitions.

If we resort for a criterion to the different principles on which different forms of government are established, we may define a republic to be, or at least may bestow that name on, a government which derives all its powers directly or indirectly from the great body of the people, and is administered by persons holding their offices during pleasure for a limited period, or during good behavior. It is *essential* to such a government that it be derived from the great body of the society, not from an inconsiderable proportion or a favored class of it; otherwise a handful of tyrannical nobles, exercising their oppressions by a delegation of their powers, might aspire to the rank of republicans and claim for their government the honorable title of republic. It is *sufficient* for such a government that the persons administering it be appointed, either directly or indirectly, by the people; and that they hold their appointments by either of the tenures just specified; otherwise every government in the United States, as well as every other popular government that has been or can be well organized or well executed, would be degraded from the republican character. According to the constitution of every State in the Union, some or other of the officers of government are appointed indirectly only by the people. According to most of them, the chief magistrate himself is so appointed. And according to one, this mode of appointment is extended to one of the co-ordinate branches of the legislature. According to all the constitutions, also, the tenure of the highest offices is extended to a definite period, and in many instances, both within the legislative and executive departments, to a period of years. According to the provisions of most of the constitutions, again, as well as according to the most respectable and received opinions on the subject, the members of the judiciary department are to retain their offices by the firm tenure of good behavior.

On comparing the Constitution planned by the convention with the standard here fixed, we perceive at once that it is, in the most rigid sense, conformable to it. The House of Representatives, like that of one branch at least of all the State legislatures, is elected immediately by the great body of the people. The Senate, like the present Congress and the Senate of Maryland, derives its appointment indirectly from the people. The President is indirectly derived from the choice of the people, according to the example in most of the States. Even the judges, with all other officers of the Union, will, as in the several States, be the choice, though a remote choice, of the people themselves. The duration of the appointments is equally conformable to the republican standard and to the model of State constitutions. The House of Representatives is periodically elective, as in all the States; and for the period of two years, as in the State of South Carolina. The Senate is elective for the period of six years, which is but one year more than the period of the Senate of Maryland, and but two more than that of the Senates of New York and Virginia. The President is to continue in office for the period of four years; as in New York and Delaware the chief magistrate is elected for three years, and in South Carolina for two years. In the other States the election is annual. In several of the States, however, no constitutional provision is made for the impeachment of the chief magistrate. And in Delaware and Virginia he is not impeachable till out of office. The President of the United States is impeachable at any time during his continuance in office. The tenure by which the judges are to hold their places is, as it unquestionably ought to be, that of good behavior. The tenure of the ministerial offices generally will be a subject of legal regulation, conformably to the reason of the case and the example of the State constitutions.

Could any further proof be required of the republican complexion of this system, the most decisive one might be found in its absolute prohibition of titles of nobility, both under the federal and the State governments; and in its express guaranty of the republican form to each of the latter.

"But it was not sufficient," say the adversaries of the proposed Constitution, "for the convention to adhere to the republican form. They ought with equal care, to have preserved the *federal* form, which regards the Union as a *Confederacy* of sovereign states; instead of which they have framed a *national* government, which regards the Union as a *consolidation* of the States." And it is asked by what authority this bold and radical innovation was undertaken? The handle which has been made of this objection requires that it should be examined with some precision.

Without inquiring into the accuracy of the distinction on which the objection is founded, it will be necessary to a just estimate of its force, first, to ascertain the real character of the government in question; secondly, to inquire how far the convention were authorized to propose such a government; and thirdly, how far the duty they owed to their country could supply any defect of regular authority.

First. In order to ascertain the real character of the government, it may be considered in relation to the foundation on which it is to be established; to the sources from which its ordinary powers are to be drawn; to the operation of those powers; to the extent of them; and to the authority by which future changes in the government are to be introduced.

On examining the first relation, it appears, on one hand, that the Constitution is to be founded on the assent and ratification of the people of America, given by deputies elected for the special purpose; but, on the other, that this assent and ratification is to be given by the people, not as individuals composing one entire nation, but as composing the distinct and independent States to which they respectively belong. It is to be the assent and ratification of the several States, derived from the supreme authority in each State, the authority of the people themselves. The act, therefore, establishing the Constitution will not be a *national*, but a *federal* act.

That it will be a federal and not a national act, as these terms are understood by the objectors; the act of the people, as forming so many independent States, not as forming one aggregate nation, is obvious from this single consideration: that it is to result neither from the decision of a *majority* of the people of the Union, nor from that of a *majority* of the States. It must result from the *unanimous* assent of the several States that are parties to it, differing no otherwise from their ordinary assent than in its being expressed, not by the legislative authority, but by that of the people themselves. Were the people regarded in this transaction as forming one nation, the will of the majority of the whole people of the United States would bind the minority, in the same manner as the majority in each State must bind the minority; and the will of the majority must be determined either by a comparison of the individual votes, or by considering the will of the majority of the States as evidence of the will of a majority of the people of the United States. Neither of these rules have been adopted. Each State, in ratifying the Constitution, is considered as a sovereign body, independent of all others, and only to be bound by its own voluntary act. In this relation, then, the new Constitution will, if established, be a *federal*, and not a *national* constitution.

The next relation is to the sources from which the ordinary powers of government are to be derived. The House of Representatives will derive its powers from the people of America; and the people will be represented in the same proportion and on the same principle as they are in the legislature of a particular State. So far the government is *national*, not *federal*. The Senate, on the other hand, will derive its powers from the States as political and coequal societies; and these will be represented on the principle of equality in the Senate, as they now are in the existing Congress. So far the government is FEDERAL, not NATIONAL. The executive power will be derived from a very compound source. The immediate election of the President is to be made by the States in their political characters. The votes allotted to them are in a compound ratio, which considers them partly as distinct and coequal societies, partly as unequal members of the same society. The eventual election, again, is to be made by that branch of the legislature which consists of the national representatives; but in this particular act they are to be thrown into the form of individual delegations, from so many distinct and coequal bodies politic. From this aspect of the government it appears to be of a mixed character, presenting at least as many *federal* as *national* features.

The difference between a federal and national government, as it relates to the *operation of the government*, is supposed to consist in this, that in the former the powers operate on the political bodies composing the Confederacy in their political capacities; in the latter, on the individual citizens composing the nation in their individual capacities. On trying the Constitution by this criterion, it falls under the NATIONAL, not the FEDERAL character; though perhaps not so completely as has been understood. In several cases, and particularly in the trial of controversies to which States may be parties, they must be viewed and proceeded against in their collective and political capacities only. But the operation of the government on the people in their individual capacities, in its ordinary and most essential proceedings, may, on the whole, designate it, in this relation, a *national* government.

But if the government be national with regard to the *operation* of its powers, it changes its aspect again when we contemplate it in relation to the extent of its powers. The idea of a national government involves in it not only an authority over the individual citizens, but an indefinite supremacy over all persons and things, so far as they are objects of lawful government. Among a people consolidated into one nation, this supremacy is completely vested in the national legislature. Among communities united for particular purposes, it is vested partly in the general and partly in the municipal legislatures. In the former case, all local authorities are subordinate to the supreme; and may be controlled, directed, or abolished by it at pleasure. In the latter, the local or municipal authorities form distinct and independent portions of the supremacy, no more subject, within their respective spheres, to the general authority than the general authority is subject to them, within its own sphere. In this relation, then, the proposed government cannot be deemed a *national* one; since its jurisdiction extends to certain enumerated objects only, and leaves to the several States a residuary and inviolable sovereignty over all other objects. It is true that in controversies relating to the boundary between the two jurisdictions, the tribunal which is ultimately to decide is to be established under the general government. But this does not change the principle of the case. The decision is to be impartially made, according to the rules of the Constitution; and all the usual and most effectual precautions are taken to secure this impartiality. Some such tribunal is clearly essential to prevent an appeal to the sword and a dissolution of the compact; and that it ought to be established under the general rather than under the local governments, or, to speak more properly, that it could be safely established under the first alone, is a position not likely to be combated.

If we try the Constitution by its last relation to the authority by which amendments are to be made, we find it neither wholly *national* nor wholly *federal*. Were it wholly national, the supreme and ultimate authority would reside in the *majority* of the people of the Union; and this authority would be competent at all times, like that of a majority of every national society to alter or abolish its established government. Were it wholly federal, on the other hand, the concurrence of each State in the Union would be essential to every alteration that would be binding on all. The mode provided by the plan of the convention is not founded on either of these principles. In requiring more than a majority, and particularly in computing the proportion by *States*, not by *citizens*, it departs from the *national* and advances towards the *federal* character; in rendering the concurrence of less than the whole number of States sufficient, it loses again the federal and partakes of the *national* character.

The proposed Constitution, therefore, is, in strictness, neither a national nor a federal Constitution, but a composition of both. In its foundation it is federal, not national; in the sources from which the ordinary powers of the government are drawn, it is partly federal and partly national; in the operation of these powers, it is national, not federal; in the extent of them, again, it is federal, not national; and, finally in the authoritative mode of introducing amendments, it is neither wholly federal nor wholly national.

PUBLIUS.

Federalist No. 48: These Departments Should Not Be So Far Separated as to Have No Constitutional Control Over Each Other[1]

PUBLIUS (JAMES MADISON) * FEBRUARY 1, 1788

IT WAS SHOWN IN THE LAST PAPER THAT THE POLITICAL apothegm there examined does not require that the legislative, executive, and judiciary departments should be wholly unconnected with each other. I shall undertake, in the next place, to show that unless these departments be so far connected and blended as to give to each a constitutional control over the others, the degree of separation which the maxim requires as essential to a free government, can never in practice be duly maintained.

It is agreed on all sides that the powers properly belonging to one of the departments ought not to be directly and completely administered by either of the other departments. It is equally evident that none of them ought to possess, directly or indirectly, an overruling influence over the others in the administration of their respective powers. It will not be denied that power is of an encroaching nature and that it ought to be effectually restrained from passing the limits assigned to it. After discriminating, therefore, in theory, the several classes of power, as they may in their nature be legislative, executive, or judiciary, the next and most difficult task is to provide some practical security for each, against the invasion of the others. What this security ought to be is the great problem to be solved.

Will it be sufficient to mark, with precision, the boundaries of these departments in the constitution of the government, and to trust to these parchment barriers against the encroaching spirit of power? This is the security which appears to have been principally relied on by the compilers of most of the American constitutions. But experience assures us that the efficacy of the provision has been greatly overrated; and that some more adequate defense is indispensably necessary for the more feeble against the more powerful members of the government. The legislative department is every where extending the sphere of its activity and drawing all power into its impetuous vortex.

The founders of our republics have so much merit for the wisdom which they have displayed that no task can be less pleasing than that of pointing out the errors into which they have fallen. A respect for truth, however, obliges us to remark that they seem never for a moment to have turned their eyes from the danger, to liberty, from the overgrown and all-grasping prerogative of an hereditary magistrate, supported and fortified by an hereditary branch of the legislative authority. They seem never to have recollected the danger from legislative usurpations, which, by assembling all power in the same hands, must lead to the same tyranny as is threatened by executive usurpations.

In a government where numerous and extensive prerogatives are placed in the hands of a hereditary monarch, the executive department is very justly regarded as the source of danger, and watched with all the jealousy which a zeal for liberty ought to inspire. In a democracy, where a multitude of people exercise in person the legislative functions and are continually exposed, by their incapacity for regular deliberation and concerted measures, to the ambitious intrigues of their executive magistrates, tyranny may well be apprehended, on some favorable emergency, to start up in the same quarter. But in a representative republic where the executive magistracy is carefully limited, both in the extent and the duration of its power; and where the legislative power is exercised by an assembly, which is inspired by a supposed influence over the people with an intrepid confidence in its own strength; which is sufficiently numerous to feel all the passions which actuate a multitude; yet not so numerous as to be incapable of pursuing the objects of its passions by means which reason prescribes; it is against the enterprising ambition of this department that the people ought to indulge all their jealousy and exhaust all their precautions.

The legislative department derives a superiority in our governments from other circumstances. Its constitutional powers being at once more extensive, and less susceptible of precise limits, it can, with the greater facility, mask, under complicated and indirect measures, the encroachments which it makes on the co-ordinate departments. It is not infrequently a question of real nicety in legislative bodies whether the operation of a particular measure will, or will not, extend beyond the legislative sphere. On the other side, the executive power being restrained within a narrower compass and being more simple in its nature, and the judiciary being described by landmarks still less uncertain, projects of usurpation by either of these departments would immediately betray and defeat themselves. Nor is this all: as the legislative department alone has access to the pockets of the people, and has in some constitutions full discretion, and in all a prevailing influence, over the pecuniary rewards of those who fill the other departments, a dependence is thus created in the latter, which gives still greater facility to encroachments of the former.

I have appealed to our own experience for the truth of what I advance on this subject. Were it necessary to verify this experience by particular proofs, they might be multiplied without end. I might collect vouchers in abundance from the records and archives of every State in the Union. But as a more concise and at the same time equally satisfactory evidence, I will refer to the example of two States, attested by two unexceptionable authorities.

The first example is that of Virginia, a State which, as we have seen, has expressly declared in its constitution that the three great departments ought not to be intermixed. The authority in support of it is Mr. Jefferson, who, besides his other advantages for remarking the operation of the government, was himself the chief magistrate of it. In order to convey fully the ideas with which his experience had impressed him on this subject, it will be necessary to quote a passage of some length from his very interesting *Notes on the State of Virginia*, p. 195. "All the powers of government, legislative, executive, and judiciary, result to the legislative body. The concentrating these in the same hands is precisely the definition of despotic government. It will be no alleviation that these powers will be exercised by a plurality of hands, and not by a single one. One hundred and seventy-three despots would surely be as oppressive as one. Let those who doubt it turn their eyes on the republic of Venice. As little will it avail us that they are chosen by ourselves. An *elective despotism* was not the government we fought for; but one which should not only be founded on free principles, but in which the powers of government should be so divided and balanced among several bodies of magistracy as that no one could transcend their legal limits without being effectually checked and restrained by the others. For this reason that convention which passed the ordinance of government laid its foundation on this basis, that the legislative, executive and judiciary departments should be separate and distinct, so that no person should exercise the powers of more than one of them at the same time. *But no barrier was provided between these several powers.* The judiciary and executive members were left dependent on the legislative for their subsistence in office, and some of them for their continuance in it. If, therefore, the legislature assumes executive and judiciary powers, no opposition is likely to be made; nor, if made, can be effectual; because in that case they may put their proceeding into the form of an act of Assembly, which will render them obligatory on the other branches. They have accordingly *in many* instances, *decided rights* which should have been left to *judiciary controversy,* and *the direction of the executive, during the whole time of their session, is becoming habitual and familiar."*

The other State which I shall take for an example is Pennsylvania; and the other authority, the Council of Censors, which assembled in the years 1783 and 1784. A part of the duty of this body, as marked out by the Constitution, was "to inquire whether the Constitution had been preserved inviolate in every part; and whether the legislative and executive branches of government had performed their duty as guardians of the people, or assumed to themselves, or exercised, other or greater powers than they are entitled to by the Constitution." In the execution of this trust, the council were necessarily led to a comparison of both the legislative and executive proceedings with the constitutional powers of these departments; and from the facts enumerated, and to the truth of most of which both sides in the council subscribed, it appears that the Constitution had been flagrantly violated by the legislature in a variety of important instances.

A great number of laws had been passed violating, without any apparent necessity, the rule requiring that all bills of a public nature shall be previously printed for the consideration of the people; although this is one of the precautions chiefly relied on by the Constitution against improper acts of the legislature.

The constitutional trial by jury had been violated and powers assumed which had not been delegated by the Constitution.

Executive powers had been usurped.

The salaries of the judges, which the Constitution expressly requires to be fixed, had been occasionally varied; and cases belonging to the judiciary department, frequently drawn within legislative cognizance and determination.

Those who wish to see the several particulars falling under each of these heads may consult the journals of the council which are in print. Some of them, it will be found, may be imputable to peculiar circumstances connected with the war; but the greater part of them may be considered as the spontaneous shoots of an ill-constituted government.

It appears, also, that the executive department had not been innocent of frequent breaches of the Constitution. There are three observations, however, which ought to be made on this head: *first*, a great proportion of the instances were either immediately produced by the necessities of the war, or recommended by Congress or the commander-in-chief; *second*, in most of the other instances they conformed either to the declared or the known sentiments of the legislative department; *third*, the executive department of Pennsylvania is distinguished from that of the other States by the number of members composing it. In this respect, it has as much affinity to a legislative assembly as to an executive council. And being at once exempt from the restraint of an individual responsibility for the acts of the body, and deriving confidence from mutual example and joint influence, unauthorized measures would, of course, be more freely hazarded, than where the executive department is administered by a single hand, or by a few hands.

The conclusion which I am warranted in drawing from these observations is that a mere demarcation on parchment of the constitutional limits of the several departments is not a sufficient guard against those encroachments which lead to a tyrannical concentration of all the powers of government in the same hands.

Federalist No. 49: Method of Guarding Against the Encroachments of Any One Department of Government by Appealing to the People Through a Convention[1]

PUBLIUS (JAMES MADISON) * FEBRUARY 2, 1788

THE AUTHOR OF THE *NOTES ON THE STATE OF VIRGINIA*, quoted in the last paper, has subjoined to that valuable work the draught of a constitution, which had been prepared in order to be laid before a convention expected to be called in 1783, by the legislature, for the establishment of a constitution for that commonwealth. The plan, like every thing from the same pen, marks a turn of thinking, original, comprehensive, and accurate; and is the more worthy of attention as it equally displays a fervent attachment to republican government and an enlightened view of the dangerous propensities against which it ought to be guarded. One of the precautions which he proposes, and on which he appears ultimately to rely as a palladium to the weaker departments of power against the invasions of the stronger, is perhaps altogether his own, and as it immediately relates to the subject of our present enquiry, ought not to be overlooked.

His proposition is "that whenever any two of the three branches of government shall concur in opinion, each by the voices of two thirds of their whole number, that a convention is necessary for altering the Constitution, or *correcting breaches of it*, a convention shall be called for the purpose."

As the people are the only legitimate fountain of power, and it is from them that the constitutional charter, under which the several branches of government hold their power, is derived, it seems strictly consonant to the republican theory to recur to the same original authority, not only whenever it may be necessary to enlarge, diminish, or new-model the powers of government; but also whenever any one of the departments may commit encroachments on the chartered authorities of the others. The several departments being perfectly co-ordinate by the terms of their common commission, neither of them, it is evident, can pretend to an exclusive or superior right of settling the boundaries between their respective powers; and how are the encroachments of the stronger to be prevented, or the wrongs of the weaker to be redressed, without an appeal to the people themselves, who, as the grantors of the commission, can alone declare its true meaning, and enforce its observance?

There is certainly great force in this reasoning, and it must be allowed to prove that a constitutional road to the decision of the people ought to be marked out and kept open, for certain great and extraordinary occasions. But there appear to be insuperable objections against the proposed recurrence to the people, as a provision in all cases for keeping the several departments of power within their constitutional limits.

In the first place, the provision does not reach the case of a combination of two of the departments against a third. If the legislative authority, which possesses so many means of operating on the motives of the other departments, should be able to gain to its interest either of the others, or even one third of its members, the remaining department could derive no advantage from this remedial provision. I do not dwell, however, on this objection, because it may be thought to lie rather against the modification of the principle, than against the principle itself.

In the next place, it may be considered as an objection inherent in the principle that as every appeal to the people would carry an implication of some defect in the government, frequent appeals would, in great measure deprive the government of that veneration which time bestows on everything, and without which perhaps the wisest and freest governments would not possess the requisite stability. If it be true that all governments rest on opinion, it is no less true that the strength of opinion in each individual, and its practical influence on his conduct, depend much on the number which he supposes to have entertained the same opinion. The reason of man, like man himself, is timid and cautious when left alone, and acquires firmness and confidence in proportion to the number with which it is associated. When the examples which fortify opinion are *ancient* as well as *numerous*, they are known to have a double effect. In a nation of philosophers, this consideration ought to be disregarded. A reverence for the laws would be sufficiently inculcated by the voice of an enlightened reason. But a nation of philosophers is as little to be expected as the philosophical race of kings wished for by Plato. And in every other nation, the most rational government will not find it a superfluous advantage to have the prejudices of the community on its side.

The danger of disturbing the public tranquility by interesting too strongly the public passions is a still more serious objection against a frequent reference of constitutional questions to the decision of the whole society. Notwithstanding the success which has attended the revisions of our established forms of government and which does so much honor to the virtue and intelligence of the people of America, it must be confessed that the experiments are of too ticklish a nature to be unnecessarily multiplied. We are to recollect that all the existing constitutions were formed in the midst of a danger which repressed the passions most unfriendly to order and concord; of an enthusiastic confidence of the people in their patriotic leaders, which stifled the ordinary diversity of opinions on great national questions; of a universal ardor for new and opposite forms, produced by a universal resentment and indignation against the ancient government; and whilst no spirit of party connected with the changes to be made, or the abuses to be reformed, could mingle its leaven in the operation. The future situations in which we must expect to be usually placed do not present any equivalent security against the danger which is apprehended.

But the greatest objection of all is that the decisions which would probably result from such appeals would not answer the purpose of maintaining the constitutional equilibrium of the government. We have seen that the tendency of republican governments is to an aggrandizement of the legislative at the expense of the other departments. The appeals to the people, therefore, would usually be made by the executive and judiciary departments. But whether made by one side or the other, would each side enjoy equal advantages on the trial? Let us view their different situations. The members of the executive and judiciary departments are few in number, and can be personally known to a small part only of the people. The latter, by the mode of their appointment, as well as by the nature and permanency of it, are too far removed from the people to share much in their prepossessions. The former are generally the objects of jealousy and their administration is always liable to be discolored and rendered unpopular. The members of the legislative department, on the other hand, are numerous. They are distributed and dwell among the people at large. Their connections of blood, of friendship, and of acquaintance embrace a great proportion of the most influential part of the society. The nature of their public trust implies a personal influence among the people, and that they are more immediately the confidential guardians of the rights and liberties of the people. With these advantages it can hardly be supposed that the adverse party would have an equal chance for a favorable issue.

But the legislative party would not only be able to plead their cause most successfully with the people. They would probably be constituted themselves the judges. The same influence which had gained them an election into the legislature would gain them a seat in the convention. If this should not be the case with all, it would probably be the case with many, and pretty certainly with those leading characters, on whom every thing depends in such bodies. The convention, in short, would be composed chiefly of men who had been, who actually were, or who expected to be, members of the department whose conduct was arraigned. They would consequently be parties to the very question to be decided by them.

It might, however, sometimes happen, that appeals would be made under circumstances less adverse to the executive and judiciary departments. The usurpations of the legislature might be so flagrant and so sudden, as to admit of no specious coloring. A strong party among themselves might take side with the other branches. The executive power might be in the hands of a peculiar favorite of the people. In such a posture of things, the public decision might be less swayed by prepossessions in favor of the legislative party. But still it could never be expected to turn on the true merits of the question. It would inevitably be connected with the spirit of preexisting parties, or of the parties springing out of the question itself. It would be connected with persons of distinguished character and extensive influence in the community. It would be pronounced by the very men who had been agents in, or opponents of, the measures to which the decision would relate. The *passions*, therefore, not the *reason*, of the public would sit in judgment. But it is the reason, alone, of the public, alone that ought to control and regulate the government. The passions ought to be controlled and regulated by the government.

We found in the last paper that mere declarations in the written

Constitution are not sufficient to restrain the several departments within their legal rights. It appears in this that occasional appeals to the people would be neither a proper nor an effectual provision for that purpose. How far the provisions of a different nature contained in the plan above quoted might be adequate I do not examine. Some of them are unquestionably founded on sound political principles, and all of them are framed with singular ingenuity and precision.

Publius

Federalist No. 51: The Structure of the Government Must Furnish the Proper Checks and Balances Between the Different Departments[1]

PUBLIUS (JAMES MADISON) * FEBRUARY 6, 1788

TO WHAT EXPEDIENT, THEN, SHALL WE FINALLY RESORT, for maintaining in practice the necessary partition of power among the several departments as laid down in the Constitution? The only answer that can be given is that as all these exterior provisions are found to be inadequate the defect must be supplied, by so contriving the interior structure of the government as that its several constituent parts may, by their mutual relations, be the means of keeping each other in their proper places. Without presuming to undertake a full development of this important idea I will hazard a few general observations which may perhaps place it in a clearer light, and enable us to form a more correct judgment of the principles and structure of the government planned by the convention.

In order to lay a due foundation for that separate and distinct exercise of the different powers of government, which to a certain extent is admitted on all hands to be essential to the preservation of liberty, it is evident that each department should have a will of its own; and consequently should be so constituted that the members of each should have as little agency as possible in the appointment of the members of the others. Were this principle rigorously adhered to, it would require that all the appointments for the supreme executive, legislative, and judiciary magistracies should be drawn from the same fountain of authority, the people, through channels having no communication whatever with one another. Perhaps such a plan of constructing the several departments would be less difficult in practice than it may in contemplation appear. Some difficulties, however, and some additional expense would attend the execution of it. Some deviations, therefore, from the principle must be admitted. In the constitution of the judiciary department in particular, it might be inexpedient to insist rigorously on the principle: first, because peculiar qualifications being essential in the members, the primary consideration ought to be to select that mode of choice which best secures these qualifications; second, because the permanent tenure by which the appointments are held in that department must soon destroy all sense of dependence on the authority conferring them.

It is equally evident that the members of each department should be as little dependent as possible on those of the others for the emoluments annexed to their offices. Were the executive magistrate, or the judges, not independent of the legislature in this particular, their independence in every other would be merely nominal.

But the great security against a gradual concentration of the several powers in the same department consists in giving to those who administer each department the necessary constitutional means and personal motives to resist encroachments of the others. The provision for defense must in this, as in all other cases, be made commensurate to the danger of attack. Ambition must be made to counteract ambition. The interest of the man must be connected with the constitutional rights of the place. It may be a reflection on human nature that such devices should be necessary to control the abuses of government. But what is government itself but the greatest of all reflections on human nature? If men were angels, no government would be necessary. If angels were to govern men, neither external nor internal controls on government would be necessary. In framing a government which is to be administered by men over men, the great difficulty lies in this: You must first enable the government to control the governed; and in the next place oblige it to control itself. A dependence on the people is, no doubt, the primary control on the government; but experience has taught mankind the necessity of auxiliary precautions.

This policy of supplying, by opposite and rival interests, the defect of better motives, might be traced through the whole system of human affairs, private as well as public. We see it particularly displayed in all the subordinate distributions of power, where the constant aim is to divide and arrange the several offices in such a manner as that each may be a check on the other—that the private interest of every individual may be a sentinel over the public rights. These inventions of prudence cannot be less requisite in the distribution of the supreme powers of the state.

But it is not possible to give to each department an equal power of self-defense. In republican government the legislative authority necessarily predominates. The remedy for this inconveniency is to divide the legislature into different branches; and to render them, by different modes of election and different principles of action, as little connected with each other as the nature of their common functions and their common dependence on the society will admit. It may even be necessary to guard against dangerous encroachments by still further precautions. As the weight of the legislative authority requires that it should be thus divided, the weakness of the executive may require, on the other hand, that it should be fortified. An absolute negative on the legislature appears, at first view, to be the natural defense with which the executive magistrate should be armed. But perhaps it would be neither altogether safe nor alone sufficient. On ordinary occasions it might not be exerted with the requisite firmness, and on extraordinary occasions it might be perfidiously abused. May not this defect of an absolute negative be supplied by some qualified connection between this weaker department and the weaker branch of the stronger department, by which the latter may be led to support the constitutional rights of the former, without being too much detached from the rights of its own department?

If the principles on which these observations are founded be just, as I persuade myself they are, and they be applied as a criterion to the several State constitutions, and to the federal Constitution, it will be found that if the latter does not perfectly correspond with them, the former are infinitely less able to bear such a test.

There are, moreover, two considerations particularly applicable to the federal system of America, which place that system in a very interesting point of view.

First. In a single republic, all the power surrendered by the people is submitted to the administration of a single government; and usurpations are guarded against by a division of the government into distinct and separate departments. In the compound republic of America, the power surrendered by the people is first divided between two distinct governments, and then the portion allotted to each subdivided among distinct and separate departments. Hence a double security arises to the rights of the people. The different governments will control each other, at the same time that each will be controlled by itself.

Second. It is of great importance in a republic not only to guard the society against the oppression of its rulers, but to guard one part of the society against the injustice of the other part. Different interests necessarily exist in different classes of citizens. If a majority be united by a common interest, the rights of the minority will be insecure. There are but two methods of providing against this evil: the one by creating a will in the community independent of the majority—that is, of the society itself; the other, by comprehending in the society so many separate descriptions of citizens as will render an unjust combination of a majority of the whole very improbable, if not impracticable. The first method prevails in all governments possessing an hereditary or self-appointed authority. This, at best, is but a precarious security; because a power independent of the society may as well espouse the unjust views of the major as the rightful interests of the minor party, and may possibly be turned against both parties. The second method will be exemplified in the federal republic of the United States. Whilst all authority in it will be derived from and dependent on the society, the society itself will be broken into so many parts, interests and classes of citizens, that the rights of individuals, or of the minority, will be in little danger from interested combinations of the majority. In a free government the security for civil rights must be the same as that for religious rights. It consists in the one case in the multiplicity of interests, and in the other in the multiplicity of sects. The degree of security in both cases will depend on the number of interests and sects; and this may be presumed to depend on the extent of country and number of people comprehended under the same government. This view of the subject must particularly recommend a proper federal system to all the sincere and considerate friends of republican government, since it shows that in exact proportion as the territory of the Union may be formed into more circumscribed Confederacies or States, oppressive combinations of a majority will be facilitated; the best security, under the republican forms, for the rights of every class of citizen, will be diminished; and consequently the stability and independence of some member of the government, the only other security, must be proportionally increased. Justice is the end of government. It is the end of civil society. It ever has been and ever will be pursued until it be obtained, or until liberty be lost in the pursuit. In a society under the forms of which the stronger faction can readily unite and oppress the weaker, anarchy may as truly be said to reign as in a state of nature, where the weaker individual is not secured against the violence of the stronger; and as, in the latter state, even the stronger individuals are prompted, by the uncertainty of their condition, to submit to a government which may protect the weak as well as themselves; so, in the former state, will the more powerful factions or parties be gradually induced, by a like motive, to wish for a government which will protect all parties, the weaker as well as the more powerful. It can be little doubted that if the State of Rhode Island was separated from the Confederacy and left to itself, the insecurity of rights under the popular form of government within such narrow limits would be displayed by such reiterated oppressions of factious majorities that some power altogether independent of the people would soon be called for by the voice of the very factions whose misrule had proved the necessity of it. In the extended republic of the United States, and among the great variety of interests, parties, and sects which it embraces, a coalition of a majority of the whole society could seldom take place on any other principles than those of justice and the general good; whilst there being thus less danger to a minor from the will of a major party, there must be less pretext, also, to provide for the security of the former, by introducing into the government a will not dependent on the latter, or, in other words, a will independent of the society itself. It is no less certain than it is important, notwithstanding the contrary opinions which have been entertained, that the larger the society, provided it lie within a practicable sphere, the more duly capable it will be of self-government. And happily for the *republican cause*, the practicable sphere may be carried to a very great extent by a judicious modification and mixture of the *federal principle*.

"Property" by James Madison[1]

MARCH 29, 1792 * *NATIONAL GAZETTE*

THIS TERM IN ITS PARTICULAR APPLICATION MEANS "THAT dominion which one man claims and exercises over the external things of the world, in exclusion of every other individual."

In its larger and juster meaning, it embraces every thing to which a man may attach a value and have a right; and which leaves to every one else the like advantage.

In the former sense, a man's land, or merchandize, or money is called his property.

In the latter sense, a man has property in his opinions and the free communication of them.

He has a property of peculiar value in his religious opinions, and in the profession and practice dictated by them.

He has a property very dear to him in the safety and liberty of his person.

He has an equal property in the free use of his faculties and free choice of the objects on which to employ them.

In a word, as a man is said to have a right to his property, he may be equally said to have a property in his rights.

Where an excess of power prevails, property of no sort is duly respected. No man is safe in his opinions, his person, his faculties, or his possessions.

Where there is an excess of liberty, the effect is the same, tho' from an opposite cause.

Government is instituted to protect property of every sort; as well that which lies in various rights of individuals, as that which the term particularly expresses. This being the end of government, that alone is a just government, which impartially secures to every man, whatever is his.

According to this standard of merit, the praise of affording a just security to property, should be sparingly bestowed on a government which, however scrupulously guarding the possessions of individuals, does not protect them in the enjoyment and communication of their opinions, in which they have an equal, and in the estimation of some, a more valuable property.

More sparingly should this praise be allowed to a government, where a man's religious rights are violated by penalties, or fettered by tests, or taxed by a hierarchy. Conscience is the most sacred of all property; other property depending in part on positive law, the exercise of that, being a natural and unalienable right. To guard a man's house as his castle, to pay public and enforce private debts with the most exact faith, can give no title to invade a man's conscience which is more sacred than his castle, or to withhold from it that debt of protection, for which the public faith is pledged, by the very nature and original conditions of the social pact.

That is not a just government, nor is property secure under it, where the property which a man has in his personal safety and personal liberty, is violated by arbitrary seizures of one class of citizens for the service of the rest. A magistrate issuing his warrants to a press gang, would be in his proper functions in Turkey or Indostan, under appellations proverbial of the most compleat despotism.

That is not a just government, nor is property secure under it, where arbitrary restrictions, exemptions, and monopolies deny to part of its citizens that free use of their faculties, and free choice of their occupations, which not only constitute their property in the general sense of the word; but are the means of acquiring property strictly called. What must be the spirit of legislation where a manufacturer of linen cloth is forbidden to bury his own child in a linen shroud, in order to favor his neighbor who manufactures woolen cloth; where the manufacturer and wearer of woolen cloth are again forbidden the economical use of buttons of that material, in favor of the manufacturer of buttons of other materials!

A just security to property is not afforded by that government, under which unequal taxes oppress one species of property and reward another species: where arbitrary taxes invade the domestic sanctuaries of the rich, and excessive taxes grind the faces of the poor; where the keenness and competitions of want are deemed an insufficient spur to labor, and taxes are again applied, by an unfeeling policy, as another spur; in violation of that sacred property, which Heaven, in decreeing man to earn his bread by the sweat of his brow, kindly reserved to him, in the small repose that could be spared from the supply of his necessities.

If there be a government then which prides itself in maintaining the inviolability of property; which provides that none shall be taken directly even for public use without indemnification to the owner, and yet directly violates the property which individuals have in their opinions, their religion, their persons, and their faculties; nay more, which indirectly violates their property, in their actual possessions, in the labor that acquires their daily subsistence, and in the hallowed remnant of time which ought to relieve their fatigues and soothe their cares, the influence will have been anticipated, that such a government is not a pattern for the United States.

If the United States mean to obtain or deserve the full praise due to wise and just governments, they will equally respect the rights of property, and the property in rights: they will rival the government that most sacredly guards the former; and by repelling its example in violating the latter, will make themselves a pattern to that and all other governments.

NOTES

Chapter 1: Eternal, Yet New

1. For an excellent study of the result that the principles set forth within the Declaration and the Constitution had on American architecture, see Allan Greenberg, *Architecture of Democracy* (New York: Rizzoli, 2006).

Chapter 2: Divide and Conquer

1. Matt Cover, "When Asked Where the Constitution Authorizes Congress to Order Americans to Buy Health Insurance, Pelosi Says: 'Are You Serious?'" CNSNews.com, October 22, 2009, http://www.cnsnews.com/node/55971. There is an audio recording of the question and answer at the Web site. One detects a note of impatience in Speaker Pelosi's voice.
2. *Congressional Record*, vol. 156, no. 43, March 21, 2010, H1896.
3. Evidence about this is ubiquitous in the Founding. See, for example, Jefferson's First Inaugural Address, given immediately upon his taking the oath to uphold the Constitution as president: "[A] wise and frugal Government, which shall restrain men from injuring one another, shall leave them otherwise free to regulate their own pursuits of industry and improvement, and shall not take from the mouth of labor the bread it has earned." Thomas Jefferson, "First Inaugural Address," March 4, 1801, in *Inaugural Addresses of the Presidents of the United States* (Washington, DC: GPO, 1989), viii, 350.
4. John C. Calhoun, "Speech on the Oregon Bill," June 27, 1848, in *The U.S. Constitution: A Reader* (Hillsdale, MI: Hillsdale College Press, 2012), 421.
5. Woodrow Wilson, "What Is Progress?" in *The U.S. Constitution: A Reader* (Hillsdale, MI: Hillsdale College Press, 2012), 640–1.
6. Edward M. House, *Philip Dru, Administrator: A Story of Tomorrow* (New York: B. W. Huebsch, 1912), 222.

7. John Dewey, "Liberalism and Social Action," in *The Papers of John Dewey: The Later Works, 1925–1953*, vol. 11, ed. Jo Ann Boydston (Carbondale: Southern Illinois University, 1987), 35.

8. Frank Goodnow, "The American Conception of Liberty," in *The U.S. Constitution: A Reader* (Hillsdale, MI: Hillsdale College Press, 2012), 630.

9. Franklin D. Roosevelt, "Commonwealth Club Address," September 23, 1932, in *The U.S. Constitution: A Reader* (Hillsdale, MI: Hillsdale College Press, 2012), 727.

10. Michael Lind, "Let's Stop Pretending the Constitution Is Sacred," *Salon*, January 4, 2011, http://www.salon.com/news/politics/war_room/2011/01/04/lind_tea_party_constitution.

11. E. J. Dionne Jr. "What a GOP Congress Might Bring," *Washington Post*, January 3, 2011,http://www.washingtonpost.com/wp-dyn/content/article/2011/01/02/AR2011010202380.html.

12. Michael Klarman, "A Skeptical View of Constitution Worship,"*Balkinization* (blog), September 27, 2010, http://balkin.blogspot.com/2010/09/skeptical-view-of-constitution-worship.html.

13. Patriotic and National Observances, Ceremonies, and Organizations, 36 U.S.C. §108 (1998).

14. Robert Bolt, *A Man for All Seasons* (New York: Vintage International, 1990), 66.

15. Sunstein stated,

> I do mean to say that at a minimum, what seems to government regulation of speech might, in some circumstances, promote free speech as understood through the democratic conception associated with both Madison and Brandeis. If so, such regulation should not be treated as a constitutionally impermissible abridgment at all. . . . [C]onsider campaign finance laws, which may well improve democratic processes by reducing the distorting effects of wealth. (Cass Sunstein, *Democracy and the Problem of Free Speech* [New York: Free Press, 1993], 35)

16. Abraham Lincoln, Fragment on the Constitution, January 1862 in *Hillsdale College Constitution Reader*, 67–68.

Chapter 3: Divorce: The Declaration and the Constitution Estranged?

1. Joseph J. Ellis, *American Creation: Triumphs and Tragedies at the Founding of the Republic* (New York: Alfred A. Knopf, 2007), 9.

2. Joseph J. Ellis, *Founding Brothers: The Revolutionary Generation* (New York: Alfred A. Knopf, 2000), 9.

3. John Lind, *An Answer to the Declaration of the American Congress* (London, 1776).

4. The Declaration is a deductive syllogism after the classic form repeated in logic books for generations (at least until the study of that subject was abandoned with the rest of the core curriculum in most places). The major

premise of such a syllogism is that all men are mortal. The minor premise: Socrates is a man. The conclusion: Socrates is mortal. The premises being true in such a syllogism, the conclusion is inescapable.

5. James Madison, "No. 63: The Senate Continued," in *The Federalist Papers*, ed. Clinton Rossiter (New York: Signet Classic, 2003), 385.

6. See James Madison, "No. 10: The Same Subject Continued": "[Pure] democracies have ever been spectacles of turbulence and contention; have ever been found incompatible with personal security or the rights of property; and have in general been as short in their lives as they have been violent in their deaths." *The Federalist Papers*, ed. Rossiter, 76. Thomas Jefferson to John Taylor, Monticello, May 28, 1816: "Such a government is evidently restrained to very narrow limits of space and population. I doubt if it would be practicable beyond the extent of a New England township. . . . [T]his pure element . . . like that of pure vital air, cannot sustain life of itself." *The Writings of Thomas Jefferson*, ed. Albert Ellery Bergh (Washington, DC: Thomas Jefferson Memorial Association, 1907), 15:19.

7. See, for example, the first anti-Federalist essay, probably written by Robert Yates of New York under the alias Brutus, in opposition to the Constitution: "No. 1: To the Citizens of the State of New York," October 18, 1787, in *The Anti-Federalist Papers and the Constitutional Convention Debates*, ed. Ralph Ketcham (New York: Signet Classic, 2003), 270–80. Brutus argues strongly that the concentration of powers in the federal government will violate the rules of Montesquieu, who wrote that republics may cover only a small extent of territory. Favoring these small republics, which he conceives the American states to be, still Brutus writes of "pure democracy":

> In a pure democracy the people are the sovereign, and their will is declared by themselves; for this purpose they must all come together to deliberate and decide. This kind of government cannot be exercised, therefore, over a country of any considerable extent; it must be confined to a single city, or at least limited to such bounds as that the people can conveniently assemble, be able to debate, understand the subject submitted to them, and declare their opinion concerning it.

8. Austen Chamberlain letter to Winston S. Churchill, December 15, 1924, in Martin Gilbert, ed, *The Churchill Documents, Volume 11, The Exchequer Years* (Hillsdale: Hillsdale College Press, 2009), 302.

9. See Colleen Sheehan, *James Madison and the Spirit of Republican Self-Government* (Cambridge: Cambridge University Press, 2009), especially chapters 4 and 5. This work is the sign of a career now matured into one of the finest contributions to our understanding of the Founding.

10. During the fifth year of the Peloponnesian War, the Athenians voted "in the fury of the moment . . . to put to death not only the prisoners at Athens, but the whole adult male population of Mytilene, and to make slaves of the women and children," but "[t]he morrow brought repentance with it

and reflection on the horrid cruelty of a decree which condemned a whole city to the fate merited only by the guilty. . . . [M]ost of the citizens wished someone to give them an opportunity for reconsidering the matter" (3.36). Thucydides, *The Landmark Thucydides*, ed. Robert B. Strassler (New York: Free Press, 1996), 175–76. Also consider "The People's" actions toward Alcibiades at 6.28–29 and 6.53, 61. Ibid., 376–77, 390, 395.

11. So far as I know, this was first noted by George Anastaplo in his book *Abraham Lincoln: A Constitutional Biography* (Lanham, MD: Rowman & Littlefield, 1999), 25.

12. Thomas Jefferson, "Draft of Instructions to the Virginia Delegates in the Continental Congress (MS Text of *A Summary View*, &c.)," July 1774, in *The Papers of Thomas Jefferson*, ed. Julian P. Boyd (Princeton: Princeton University Press, 1950–92), 1:134.

Chapter 4: The Laws of Nature and of Nature's God

1. Jeremy Black, *George III: America's Last King* (New Haven: Yale University Press, 2006), 128.

2. Ibid., 137, 148. Also see ibid., illustration 13, *Affability* by James Gillray (1795).

3. John Brooke, *King George III* (New York: McGraw-Hill, 1972), 90.

4. Manfred S. Guttmacher, *America's Last King: An Interpretation of the Madness of George III* (New York: Charles Scribner's Sons, 1941), 186–87.

5. See, for example, the Townshend duties. A good source for information on this topic is John C. Miller, *Origins of the American Revolution* (Stanford: Stanford University Press, 1943), 242–58.

6. Daniel Dulany, *Considerations on the Propriety of Imposing Taxes in the British Colonies for the Purpose of Raising a Revenue by Act of Parliament* (Annapolis, 1765), 15.

7. Olive Branch Petititon, Worthington C. Ford, et al, ed, *Journals of the Continental Congress, 1774-1789* (Washington, DC: 1904-37), 2:158–62.

8. Thomas Aquinas, *Summa Theologica*, II–I q. 91, a. 2.

9. Thomas Aquinas, *Summa Theologica*, I–I, q. 16, a. 8.

10. Jane Austen, *Pride and Prejudice* (New York: Alfred A. Knopf, 1991), 51.

11. I owe this example and much of my understanding of the thing it illustrates to a great teacher, Harry Jaffa, who has always been rightly proud of his literary education and more proud of the philosophic pursuits that have elevated and informed it.

12. Cicero, "On the Commonwealth," in *The U.S. Constitution: A Reader* (Hillsdale, MI: Hillsdale College Press, 2012), 29.

13. Alexander Hamilton, "The Farmer Refuted," February 23, 1775, in *The Papers of Alexander Hamilton: Volume 1, 1768–1778*, ed. Harold Coffin Syrett (New York: Columbia University Press, 1961–87), 122.

Chapter 5: That All Men Are Created Equal

1. These examples are accurate descriptions of two recent graduates of Hillsdale College, where I work.
2. The writings of Harry Jaffa, including those mentioned at the end of this book, are insightful in ways that few can attain on this and all related points. See especially his "Equality as a Conservative Principle," in *How to Think About the American Revolution: A Bicentennial Celebration* (Durham, NC: Carolina Academic Press, 1978), 13ff.
3. Ibid.
4. This event was well covered in the press. An Associated Press story, "Pig Flies First Class Across U.S.," appeared in the *Washington Post*, October 27, 2000, and is available at this writing on the Internet.
5. Abraham Lincoln, "Speech at Peoria, Illinois," October 16, 1854, in *The Collected Works of Abraham Lincoln: Volume II, 1848–1858*, ed. Roy P. Basler (New Brunswick, NJ: Rutgers University Press, 1953), 264.
6. Winston S. Churchill, *The Second World War: Volume IV, The Hinge of Fate* (Boston: Houghton Mifflin, 1950), 498–99.
7. Thomas Jefferson, "Letter to Roger C. Weightman," June 24, 1826, in *The U.S. Constitution: A Reader* (Hillsdale, MI: Hillsdale College Press, 2012), 109–10.
8. James Madison, "No. 10: The Same Subject Continued," in *The Federalist Papers*, ed. Rossiter, 78.
9. Abraham Lincoln, "Address before the Wisconsin State Agricultural Society, Milwaukee, Wisconsin," September 30, 1859, in *The Collected Works of Abraham Lincoln: Volume III, 1858–1860*, ed. Roy P. Basler (New Brunswick, NJ: Rutgers University Press, 1953), 479–80.
10. James Madison, "No. 51: The Structure of the Government Must Furnish the Proper Checks and Balances Between the Different Departments," in *The Federalist Papers*, ed. Clinton Rossiter (New York: Signet Classic, 2003), 319.
11. Franklin D. Roosevelt, "Democratic Convention Address." June 27, 1936, in *The U.S. Constitution: A Reader* (Hillsdale, MI: Hillsdale College Press, 2012), 734.
12. Franklin D. Roosevelt, "Commonwealth Club Address," September 23, 1932, in *The U.S. Constitution: A Reader* (Hillsdale, MI: Hillsdale College Press, 2011), 724. For an interpretation of the speech and how it came to be written, see Robert Eden, "On the Origins of the Regime of Pragmatic Liberalism: John Dewey, Adolf A. Berle, and FDR's Commonwealth Club Address of 1932," *Studies in American Political Development* 7 (Spring 1993): 74–150. Also see Ronald J. Pestritto, "Founding Liberalism, Progressive Liberalism, and the Rights of Property," *Social Philosophy and Policy* 28, no. 2 (2011): 56–73.
13. Franklin D. Roosevelt, "Annual Message to Congress," January 11, 1944, in *The U.S. Constitution: A Reader* (Hillsdale, MI: Hillsdale College Press, 2012), 745.

14. Roosevelt, "Democratic Convention Address," 733-4.
15. Roosevelt, "Annual Message to Congress," 745.
16. These arguments are documented and summarized in Ronald J. Pestritto, "The Progressive Origins of the Administrative State: Wilson, Goodnow, and Landis," *Social Philosophy and Policy* 24 (2007): 16–54
17. James Madison, "No. 10: The Same Subject Continued," in *The Federalist Papers*, ed. Rossiter, 73.
18. James Madison, "On Property," March 29, 1792, in *Hillsdale Constitution Reader*, 155.
19. "I do mean to say that at a minimum, what seems to be government regulation of speech might, in some circumstances, promote free speech as understood through the democratic conception associated with both Madison and Brandeis. If so, such regulation should not be treated as a constitutionally impermissible abridgment at all." Cass Sunstein, *Democracy and the Problem of Free Speech* (New York: Free Press, 1995), 35.
20. For more information on this topic, see Thomas G. West, "The Economic Principles of America's Founders, Property Rights, Free Markets, and Sound Money," August 30, 2010, *The Heritage Foundation First Principles Series* Report #32; and Thomas G. West, "Poverty and the Welfare State," in *Moral Ideas for America*, ed. Larry Arnn and Douglas Jeffrey (Claremont, CA: Claremont Institute, 1993), 51–72.
21. Abraham Lincoln, "Speech to One Hundred Sixty-Sixth Ohio Regiment," in *The Collected Works of Abraham Lincoln: Volume VII, 1863–1864*, ed. Roy P. Basler (New Brunswick, NJ: Rutgers University Press, 1953), 512.

Chapter 6: Hypocrisy

1. The terms slave and slavery do not occur in the Constitution, but there are three references that refer to the institution. Article I, section 2, provides that "three fifths of all other Persons" will be counted in representation and taxation. This means that the representation and taxation of slave states were increased by three-fifths of a person for each slave.

   Article I, section 9, provides that "The Migration or Importation of such Persons as any of the States now existing shall think proper to admit, shall not be prohibited by the Congress prior to the Year one thousand eight hundred and eight, but a Tax or duty may be imposed on such Importation, not exceeding ten dollars for each Person." This has to do with the importation of slaves, with the notorious slave trade. Under the Articles of Confederation, this importation was permitted indefinitely. Under the Constitution, it was guaranteed to continue for twenty years and was in fact abolished at the end of those twenty years.

   Article IV, section 2, provides that "No Person held to Service or Labour in one State, under the Laws thereof, escaping into another, shall, in Consequence of any Law or Regulation therein, be discharged from such Service or Labour, but shall be delivered up on Claim of the Party to whom such Service or Labour may be due." This, one of the most troubling features of the Constitution, involved the free states in returning escaped slaves to their masters. This produced friction for a generation and was a bone of contention right up to the outbreak of the Civil War.

2. David Armitage, *The Declaration of Independence: A Global History* (Cambridge, MA: Harvard University Press, 2007), 75. There is also an intriguing section of the reply written by Jeremy Bentham, the ancestor of modern utilitarians, critical of the theory of the Declaration. Text of Bentham's response can be found in ibid., 173–86.
3. John Lind, *An Answer to the Declaration of the American Congress* (London, 1776), 107.
4. A compromise in the Constitution provided that it would not be abolished for twenty years after the ratification of the Constitution, and it was abolished in the twentieth year, when Thomas Jefferson signed the bill to make it law.
5. Jim Powell, *Greatest Emancipations: How the West Abolished Slavery* (New York: Palgrave MacMillian, 2008), 19. For the fine story of British abolition of the slave trade in the 19th century, see William Hague, *William Wilberforce: The Life of the Great Anti-Slave Trade Campaigner* (London: Harcourt, Inc, 2007), 355–6.
6. It read:

He has waged cruel war against human nature itself, violating its most sacred rights of life and liberty in the persons of a distant people who never offended him, captivating & carrying them into slavery in another hemisphere or to incur miserable death in their transportation thither. This piratical warfare, the opprobrium of infidel powers, is the warfare of the Christian King of Great Britain. Determined to keep open a market where Men should be bought & sold, he has prostituted his negative for suppressing every legislative attempt to prohibit or restrain this execrable commerce. And that this assemblage of horrors might want no fact of distinguished die, he is now exciting those very people to rise in arms among us, and to purchase that liberty of which he has deprived them, by murdering the people on whom he has obtruded them: thus paying off former crimes committed again the Liberties of one people, with crimes which he urges them to commit against the lives of another. (Thomas Jefferson, "Draft of the Declaration of Independence," in *The U.S. Constitution: A Reader* (Hillsdale, MI: Hillsdale College Press, 2012), 397.)

7. For the relevant evidence and a knowledgeable interpretation of it, see R. B. Bernstein, *Thomas Jefferson* (Oxford: Oxford University Press, 2003), 194–98, and Paul A. Rahe, "Final Report of the Scholars Commission on the Jefferson-Hemings Matter," Thomas Jefferson Heritage Society, http://www.tjheritage.org/newscomfiles/SCReport1.pdf,35–37.

8. Along with the Declaration of Independence, the Articles of Confederation, and the Constitution of the United States. For a history and analysis of "The Organic Laws of the United States of America," see Richard H. Cox, introduction to *Four Pillars of Constitutionalism: The Organic Laws of the United States* (Amherst, NY: Prometheus Books, 1998), 9–71.

9. The Northwest Ordinance, in *The U.S. Constitution: A Reader* (Hillsdale, MI: Hillsdale College Press, 2012), 127.

10. Abraham Lincoln, "Speech at Peoria, Illinois," October 16, 1854, in *The Collected Works of Abraham Lincoln: Volume II, 1848–1858*, ed. Roy P. Basler (New Brunswick, NJ: Rutgers University Press, 1953), 249–50.

11. Thomas Jefferson, "Notes on the State of Virginia," in *Thomas Jefferson: Writings*, 288.

12. Abraham Lincoln, "Second Inaugural Address," March 4, 1865, in *The U.S. Constitution: A Reader* (Hillsdale, MI: Hillsdale College Press, 2012), 614.

13. See the letter from George Washington to Robert Morris, dated April 12, 1786: "I can only say that there is not a man living who wishes more sincerely than I do, to see a plan adopted for the abolition of it [slavery]—but there is only one proper and effectual mode by which it can be accomplished, & that is by Legislative authority: and this, as far as my suffrage will go, shall never be wanting." *The Writings of George Washington*, vol. 28, ed. John C. Fitzpatrick (Washington, DC: United States Government Printing Office, 1938), 408. John C. Hamilton, *History of the Republic of the United States of America as traced in the Writings of Alexander Hamilton and of his Contemporaries*, vol. 4 (New York: D. Appleton & Co., 1859), 439–42, for a compilation of quotations from Alexander Hamilton's works on the evils of slavery, including, "I consider civil liberty, in a genuine unadulterated sense, as the greatest of terrestrial blessings. I am convinced that the whole HUMAN RACE, is entitled to it; and, that it can be wrested from no part of them, without the blackest and most aggravated guilt" (440). Ralph Ketcham, *James Madison: A Biography* (New York: Macmillan, 1971), 148–49, and Robert Allan Rutland, *James Madison: The Founding Father* (New York: Macmillan, 1987), 70–71, 239–42, for Madison's thoughts on the institution and emancipation; and David McCullough, *John Adams* (New York: Simon & Schuster, 2001), 132–34 for John Adams's denunciation of slavery as "an evil of colossal magnitude," as well as strong statements by Benjamin Rush and James Otis. Both Hamilton and Madison suggested enlisting slaves as soldiers during the Revolutionary War in exchange for their freedom. In 1781 New York passed an act by which slaves could earn their freedom with three years of military service. Hamilton, *History of the Republic*, 441. Many of these statements and others are reprinted in *The U.S. Constitution: A Reader* (Hillsdale, MI: Hillsdale College Press, 2012), 401–2.

14. Thomas G. West, *Vindicating the Founders: Race, Sex, Class, and Justice in the Origins of America* (Lanham, MD: Rowman and Littlefield, 1997), 14.

15. John Jay, "Letter to the English Anti-Slavery Society for the Manumission

of Slaves," June 1788, in *The U.S. Constitution: A Reader* (Hillsdale, MI: Hillsdale College Press, 2012), 410.

16. Abraham Lincoln, "Seventh Lincoln-Douglas Debate," Alton, Illinois, October 15, 1858, in *The U.S. Constitution: A Reader* (Hillsdale, MI: Hillsdale College Press, 2012), 528–9.

17. John C. Calhoun, *Disquisition on Government*, in *Union and Liberty: The Political Philosophy of John C. Calhoun*, ed. Ross M. Lence (Indianapolis: Liberty Fund, 1992), 66.

18. For Calhoun, this is a not a fact of nature; there do not seem to be any facts of nature of this kind. He holds rather that "in the present state of civilization, where two races of different origin, and distinguished by color, and other physical differences, as well as intellectual, are brought together, the relation now existing in the slaveholding States between the two, is, instead of an evil, a good—a positive good." Calhoun, "Speech on the Reception of Abolition Petitions," February 6, 1837, in *The U.S. Constitution: A Reader* (Hillsdale, MI: Hillsdale College Press, 2012), 417. He leaves open the possibility that the "present state of civilization" will be succeeded by another state.

19. Alexander Stephens, "Cornerstones Speech," March 12, 1861, in *The U.S. Constitution: A Reader* (Hillsdale, MI: Hillsdale College Press, 2012), 579.

20. Abraham Lincoln, "Second Inaugural Address," March 4, 1865, in *The U.S. Constitution: A Reader* (Hillsdale, MI: Hillsdale College Press, 2012), 614.

21. Abraham Lincoln, "Speech on the Dred Scott Decision," June 26, 1857, in *The U.S. Constitution: A Reader* (Hillsdale, MI: Hillsdale College Press, 2011), 508.

Chapter 7: The Marriage of Many Causes

1. Alexander Hamilton, "No. 1: General Introduction," in *The Federalist Papers*, ed. Clinton Rossiter (New York: Signet Classic, 2003), 27.

2. James Madison, "No. 39: The Conformity of the Plan to Republican Principles," in *The Federalist Papers*, ed. Rossiter, 236.

3. Winston S. Churchill, *Marlborough: His Life and Times* (London: George G. Harrap & Co., 1933), 1:169. Here Churchill describes the extraordinary ability of the greatest generals. In other works he associates that ability with that of the greatest artists, philosophers, and orators. See his "Painting as a Pastime," in *Thoughts and Adventures: Churchill Reflects on Spies, Cartoons, Flying, and the Future*, ed. James W. Muller (Wilmington, DE: ISI Books, 2009), beginning p. 323.

4. Of his work on the ceiling of the Sistine Chapel, Michelangelo said, "After four tortured years, more than 400 over life-sized figures, I felt as old and as weary as Jeremiah. I was only 37, yet friends did not recognize the old man I had become." Quoted in John Barbour, *The Road from Eden: Studies in Christianity and Culture* (Palo Alto: Academica Press, 2008), 221.

5. George Washington wrote,

This army, the main American Army, will certainly not suffer itself to be out done by their northern Brethren [General Gates's army]; they will never endure such disgrace; but with an ambition becoming free-men, contending in the most righteous cause rival the heroic spirit which swelled their bosoms, and which, so nobly exerted has procured them deathless renown. Covet! my Countrymen, and fellow soldiers! Covet! a share of the glory due to heroic deeds! Let it never be said, that in a day of action, you turned your backs on the foe; let the enemy no longer triumph. (George Washington's General Orders, October 3, 1777, in Robert Middlekauff, *The Glorious Cause: The American Revolution 1763-1789* [Oxford: Oxford University Press, 2005], 397)

6. John Marshall, *Life of Washington* (Philadelphia, 1804–7), 2:57.
7. James Madison, "No. 40: The Powers of the Convention to Form a Mixed Government Examined and Sustained," in *The Federalist Papers*, ed. Rossiter, 253.
8. Madison, "No. 39," *Federalist Papers*, 236.
9. James Madison, "No. 10: The Same Subject Continued," in *The Federalist Papers*, ed. Rossiter, 76.
10. Madison, "No. 39," *Federalist Papers*, 236.
11. Ibid.
12. Ibid.
13. George Mason, "The Virginia Declaration of Rights," June 12, 1776, in *The U.S. Constitution: A Reader* (Hillsdale, MI: Hillsdale College Press, 2012), 115.
14. Ibid., 116.
15. Ibid., 117.
16. Pauline Maier, *Ratification: The People Debate the Constitution, 1787–1788* (New York: Simon & Schuster, 2010), 138–41.
17. John Adams, "Massachusetts Bill of Rights, 1780," in *Documents of American History*, ed. Henry S. Commager (New York: Appleton-Century-Crofts, 1963), 107.
18. Ibid.
19. Ibid.
20. "For Forms of Government let fools contest; / Whate'er is best administer'd is best." Alexander Pope, "An Essay on Man in Four Epistles," Epistle III, ll. 303–4, in *Pope Poetical Works*, ed. Herbert Davis (Oxford: Oxford University Press, 1983), 267. Alexander Hamilton also quotes these lines in "No. 68: The Mode of Electing the President," in *The Federalist Papers*, ed. Rossiter, 413. There he calls them a heresy and then reverses the point. A government of good form, he says, will have an "aptitude and tendency to produce good administration."
21. John Adams, "Thoughts on Government, Applicable to the Present State of the American Colonies," in *John Adams: Revolutionary Writings, 1775–1783*, ed. Gordon Wood (New York: Literary Classics of the United States, 2011), 49.

22. Ibid.
23. Ibid., 50.
24. Hamilton, "No. 1," *Federalist Papers*, 27.

Chapter 8: The Soul Writ Large

1. James Madison, "Vices of the Political System of the United States," in *The Papers of James Madison*, ed. Robert A. Rutland (Chicago: University of Chicago Press, 1975), 9:348–58.
2. Ibid., 354–55.
3. Ibid., 355.
4. James Madison, "No. 10: The Same Subject Continued," in *The Federalist Papers*, ed. Clinton Rossiter (New York: Signet Classic, 2003), 79.
5. James Madison, "No. 63: The Senate Continued," in *The Federalist Papers*, ed. Rossiter, 385.
6. My attention was first called to this phrase, its meaning and importance, by Charles Kesler many years ago, in my relative youth and his greater youth. He discovered it and much more about the *Federalist* to the great excitement of his friends. He is now the editor of the standard edition of *The Federalist Papers* (New York: Signet Classic, 2003) and of several other works listed in the bibliography.
7. Madison, "No. 10," *Federalist Papers*, 73.
8. Ibid., 74.
9. James Madison, "No. 55: The Total Number of the House of Representatives," in *The Federalist Papers*, ed. Rossiter, 343.
10. Madison, "No. 10," *Federalist Papers*, 73.
11. Of the necessity of republican government (representative government deriving its powers from the "great body" of the people), Madison writes, "[O]therwise a handful of tyrannical nobles, exercising their oppressions by a delegation of their powers, might aspire to the rank of republicans and claim for their government the honorable title of republic." "No. 39," *Federalist Papers*, 237. Again, in *Federalist* 51:

    [C]reating a will in the community independent of the majority . . . prevails in all governments possessing an hereditary or self-appointed authority. This, at best, is but a precarious security; because a power independent of the society may as well espouse the unjust views of the major as the rightful interests of the minor party, and may possibly be turned against both parties. ("No. 51," Federalist Papers, 320–21).

12. James Madison, "No. 51: The Structure of the Government Must Furnish the Proper Checks and Balances Between the Different Departments," in *The Federalist Papers*, ed. Rossiter, 317–18.
13. Madison, "No. 10," *Federalist Papers*, 76.
14. Ibid., 75. Here we have an indirect reference to a famous passage in Plato.

There will be a direct one, made in reference not to statesmen but to citizens, soon enough. Plato, *The Republic*, trans. Allan Bloom (New York: Basic Books, 1968), 488a-e.

15. Thomas Jefferson, letter to George Rogers Clark, Richmond, December 25, 1780, in *The Papers of Thomas Jefferson*, ed. Julian P. Boyd (Princeton: Princeton University Press, 1951), 4:237.

16. Alexander Hamilton, "No. 1: General Introduction," in *The Federalist Papers*, ed. Rossiter, 27.

17. For an exploration of representation and how it makes all the other devices of constitutional rule possible, see Charles Kesler, introduction and notes to *The Federalist Papers*, ed. Clinton Rossiter (New York: Signet Classic, 2003).

18. Madison, "No. 10," *Federalist Papers*, 78.

19. Adam Smith, *An Inquiry into the Nature and Causes of the Wealth of Nations* (Washington, DC: Regnery, 1998), 513. In another place in the book Smith writes the famous passage: "It is not from the benevolence of the butcher, the brewer, or the baker, that we can expect our dinner, but from their regard to their own interest" (14).

20. Madison, "No. 10," *Federalist Papers*, 78. Also see Colleen Sheehan, *James Madison and the Spirit of Republican Self-Government* (Cambridge: Cambridge University Press, 2009), 88.

21. Madison, "No. 10," *Federalist Papers*, 77–8.

22. Madison, "No. 51," *Federalist Papers*, 320.

23. Article 5 concerns the amendment process; Article 6, the transition from the articles of Confederation to the Constitution; Article 7, ratification.

24. Madison, "No. 51," *Federalist Papers*, 317–18.

25. James Madison, "No. 48: These Departments Should Not Be So Far Separated as to Have No Constitutional Control Over Each Other," in *The Federalist Papers*, ed. Rossiter, 306.

26. Publius is concerned that the branch of the government closest to the sovereign people will tend to dominate the other branches. That is why Hamilton thinks the judiciary is the "least dangerous" branch. "No. 78: The Judiciary Department," *The Federalist Papers*, ed. Rossiter, 463–71. That is also why it is necessary to divide the legislature into two houses. Madison, "No. 51," Federalist Papers, 317–22; and John Adams, "Thoughts on Government, Applicable to the Present State of the American Colonies," in *John Adams: Revolutionary Writings*, 1775–1783, ed. Gordon Wood (New York: Literary Classics of the United States, 2011), 49–56.

27. Madison, "No. 48," *Federalist Papers*, 305.

28. Thomas Jefferson, "Notes on the State of Virginia," in *Thomas Jefferson: Writings*, ed. Merrill D. Peterson (New York: Library of America, 1984), 245.

29. Madison, "No. 48," *Federalist Papers*, 305.

30. Madison, "No. 51," *Federalist Papers*, 319.

31. Ibid.

32. James Madison, "No. 49: Method of Guarding Against the Encroachments of Any One Department of Government by Appealing to the People Through a Convention," in *The Federalist Papers*, ed. Rossiter, 310.
33. Ibid., 311.
34. Ibid.
35. Ibid., 311–12.
36. Plato, *The Republic*, 488 a-e.
37. Madison, "No. 49," *Federalist Papers*, 312.
38. Ibid., 314.
39. Aristotle, *Nicomachean Ethics*, trans. Joe Sachs (Newbury, MA: Focus Publishing, 2002), 1098 a12.
40. George Washington, "The First Inaugural Address," in *The Writings of Washington*, ed. John. C. Fitzpatrick (Washington, DC: United States Printing Office, 1939), 30:294.
41. Colleen Sheehan, *James Madison and the Spirit of Republican Self-Government* (Cambridge: Cambridge University Press, 2009), xv.
42. Winston S. Churchill, *Marlborough: His Life and Times* (London: George G. Harrap & Co., 1933), 1:169.

Conclusion

1. Woodrow Wilson, "The Study of Administration," in *The U.S. Constitution: A Reader* (Hillsdale, MI: Hillsdale College Press, 2012), 664.
2. John Dewey, "The Crisis of Liberalism," in *Liberalism and Social Action* (New York: Capricorn Books, 1935), 48.
3. Frank Goodnow, "The American Conception of Liberty," in *The U.S. Constitution: A Reader* (Hillsdale, MI: Hillsdale College Press, 2012), 632.
4. Ibid., 633–4.
5. For a documented discussion of these points, see Ronald J. Pestritto, "The Progressive Origins of the Administrative State: Wilson, Goodnow, and Landis," *Social Philosophy and Policy* 24 (2007), 16–54.
6. Ibid.
7. "New Low: 17% Say U.S. Government Has Consent of the Governed," Rasmussen Reports, August 7, 2011, http://www.rasmussenreports.com.
8. Abraham Lincoln, "Speech on the Dred Scott Decision," June 26, 1857, in *The U.S. Constitution: A Reader* (Hillsdale, MI: Hillsdale College Press, 2012), 508.
9. For an excellent discussion of these points about local government and the American constitutional system, see Paul A. Rahe, *Soft Despotism, Democracy's Drift: Montesquieu, Rousseau, Tocqueville & the Modern Project* (New Haven: Yale University Press, 2009).
10. Alexis de Tocqueville, *Democracy in America*, trans. Harvey C. Mansfield and Delba Winthrop (Chicago: University of Chicago Press, 1992), 87. Of private associations, he writes,

The political associations that exist in the United States form only a detail in the midst of the immense picture that sum of associations presents there. Americans of all ages, all conditions, all minds constantly unite. Not only do they have also have a thousand other kinds: religious, moral, grave, futile, very general and very particular, immense and very small; Americans use associations to give fêtes, to found seminaries, to build inns, to raise churches, to distribute books, to send missionaries to the antipodes; in this manner they create hospitals, prisons, schools. Finally, if it is a question of bringing to light a truth or developing a sentiment with the support of a great example, they associate. Everywhere that, at the head of a new undertaking, you see the government in France and a great lord in England, count on it that you will perceive an association in the United States. *Democracy in America*, 489.

11. Ibid., 90.
12. Ibid.
13. See Thomas G. West, "Poverty and the Welfare State" (paper, Claremont Institute, February 1993).
14. See Richard Epstein, *Supreme Neglect: How to Revive Constitutional Protection for Private Property* (New York: Oxford University Press, 2008).
15. James Madison, "No. 62: The Senate," in *The Federalist Papers*, ed. Rossiter, 379.
16. Now the states of Ohio, Indiana, Michigan, Illinois, Wisconsin, and the northeastern part of Minnesota.

Appendix I
1. The Declaration of Independence, http://www.archives.gov/exhibits/charters/declaration_transcript.html

Appendix II
1. The Constitution of the United States, http://www.archives.gov/exhibits/charters/constitution.html

Appendixes III–VII
1. *The Federalist Papers*, http://thomas.loc.gov/home/histdox/fedpapers.html

Appendix VIII
1. James Madison, "Property," *The Writings of James Madison: 1790-1802*, Volume VI, 1790-1802 (Putnam: NY, 1906), 101–103.

Suggested Further Reading

Ellis, Joseph J. *American Creation: Triumphs and Tragedies at the Founding of the Republic*. New York: Alfred A. Knopf, 2007.

———. *Founding Brothers: The Revolutionary Generation*. New York: Alfred A. Knopf, 2000.

Erler, Edward J. *The American Polity: Essays on the Theory and Practice of Constitutional Government*. New York: Crane Russak, 1991.

Gilbert, Sir Martin. *The Will of the People: Churchill and Parliamentary Democracy*. Toronto, CA: Random House of Canada, 2006.

Jaffa, Harry V. *American Conservatism and the American Founding*. Durham, NC: Carolina Academic Press, 1984.

———. *The Conditions of Freedom: Essays in Political Philosophy*. Claremont, CA: Claremont Institute, 1999.

———. *Crisis of the House Divided*. Garden City, NY: Doubleday, 1959.

———. *Equality and Liberty: Theory and Practice in American Politics*. Claremont, CA: Claremont Institute, 1999.

———. *A New Birth of Freedom: Abraham Lincoln and the Coming of the Civil War*.Lanham, MD: Rowman & Littlefield, 2000.

———. *Storm Over the Constitution*. Lanham, MD: Lexington Books, 1999.

Jaffa, Harry V., with Bruce Ledewitz, Robert L. Stone, and George Anastaplo. *Original Intent & The Framers of the Constitution: A Disputed Question*. Washington, DC: Regnery Gateway, 1994.

Jones, Gordon S., and John A. Marini, eds. *The Imperial Congress: Crisis in the Separation of Powers*. New York: Pharos Books, 1988.

Kesler, Charles. Introduction and notes to *The Federalist Papers*. Edited by Clinton Rossiter. New York: Signet Classic, 2003.

———, ed. *Saving the Revolution: The Federalist Papers and the American Founding*. New York: Free Press, 1987.

Marini, John A., and Ken Masugi, eds. *The Progressive Revolution in Politics and Political Science: Transforming the American Regime*. Lanham, MD: Rowman & Littlefield, 2005.

Pestritto, Ronald J. *Woodrow Wilson and the Roots of Modern Liberalism*. Lanham, MD: Rowman & Littlefield, 2005.

Pestritto, Ronald J., and Thomas G. West, eds. *The American Founding and the Social Compact*. Lanham, MD: Lexington Books, 2003.

Pestritto, Ronald J., and Thomas G. West. *Challenges to the American Founding: Slavery, Historicism, and Progressivism in the Nineteenth Century*. Lanham, MD: Lexington Books, 2005.

Pestritto, Ronald J., and Thomas G. West, eds. *Modern America and the Legacy of the Founding*. Lanham, MD: Lexington Books, 2006.

Rahe, Paul A. *Montesquieu and the Logic of Liberty: War, Religion, Commerce, Climate, Terrain, Technology, Uneasiness of Mind, the Spirit of Political Vigilance, and the Foundations of the Modern Republic*. New Haven: Yale University Press, 2009.

———. *Republics Ancient and Modern: Classical Republicanism and the American Revolution*. Chapel Hill: University of North Carolina Press, 1992.

———. *Soft Despotism, Democracy's Drift: Montesquieu, Rousseau, Tocqueville, and the Modern Prospect*. New Haven: Yale University Press, 2009.

Schmitt, Gary J., and Robert H. Webking. "Revolutionaries, Antifederalists, and Federalists: Comments on Gordon Wood's Understanding of the American Founding." *The Political Science Reviewer* 9 (1979): 195–229.

Sheehan, Colleen A. *James Madison and the Spirit of Republican Self-Government*. New York: Cambridge University Press, 2009.

Silver, Thomas B. *Coolidge and the Historians*. Durham, NC: Carolina Academic Press, 1983.

Spalding, Matthew. *We Still Hold These Truths: Rediscovering Our Principles, Reclaiming Our Future*. Wilmington, DE: ISI Books, 2009.

The U.S. Constitution: A Reader. Hillsdale, MI: Hillsdale College Press, 2012.

West, Thomas G. *Vindicating the Founders: Race, Sex, Class, and Justice in the Origins of America*. Lanham, MD: Rowman & Littlefield, 1997.

Wood, Gordon. *The Creation of the American Republic*. Chapel Hill: University of North Carolina Press, 1969.

ACKNOWLEDGMENTS

I HAVE BEEN FORTUNATE TO KNOW MANY STUDENTS OF high ability. Some of the best of them have worked skillfully and often into the night to make this book more accurate and to improve its judgments. They begin with Cody Strecker, who set a high standard over more than a year of toil on this and other writing projects with me. Also they include Kyle Murnen, Alice Arnn, Kathleen Arnn, Natalie Mock, Victoria Bergen, Heather Shiner, and Kevin Bishop. I thank them for the skill and the fun they bring to the work. The chief of staff in the office, Mike Harner, enjoys them as much as I, and he keeps them organized with the same skill he brings to projects all over the college.

Stephen Smith, a colleague on the Hillsdale College faculty, made comments on the section concerning Sir Thomas More. He is one of many teachers here who has taught me things that I value deeply. I have the privilege of teaching the Constitution here at Hillsdale. The students I have in class, and others I speak with about the campus, inspire me more than I can do for them. I thank them.

I am blessed by my friends and teachers, and they overlap so much and for so long that I have trouble remembering who thought of what in our long relationship. Several of them have written better than I on the subject of this book, and I have mentioned their works in many endnotes and in the list of readings at the end. They include Charles R. Kesler, Thomas G. West, Edward Erler, John Marini, Ronald J. Pestritto, Colleen Sheehan, Paul Rahe, Matthew Spalding, and the late Thomas B. Silver. One who is so grand that I cannot call him a friend is Harry V. Jaffa, without whom we Americans would know much less about our country or ourselves than we know. I have studied Winston Churchill for many years. From him and from my teacher, the Churchill biographer Sir Martin Gilbert, I have learned the vital fact that statesmanship and constitutionalism are necessary companions. There are doubtless mistakes in this book, and these people are best qualified to correct them. I thank them in advance.

Douglas Jeffrey has been reading and editing things I have written for the better part of thirty years. He is the editor, for example, of *A New Birth of Freedom* by Harry Jaffa, and he is a master of that craft as well as a friend and colleague. I thank also my and Doug's other colleagues who together manage Hillsdale College. Their complex duties have been heavier while I have been working on this book, and they have discharged them as always without complaint or failure.

Kristen Parrish of Thomas Nelson came to see me to urge the writing of this book. A few days ago, thinking I would never finish, I was blaming her. Now that it is done I express my gratitude. Her colleague, Joel Miller, could not make that first trip, laid up with a broken leg. The two of them are delightful, and now Joel is healed.

I thank the people for whom I work, the trustees of Hillsdale College, their Chairman Bill Brodbeck, and their Vice Chairman Pat Sajak. In addition to the guidance and support they give me, I thank them for the worthiness with which they carry the responsibility for this old and good place. They are not quite so much fun to work with as students, but almost.

The girl I married more than thirty years ago is a friend and an example to me, and she has helped with this task as she does with everything. Penny and our children are the first cause and purpose of any good I do.

ABOUT THE AUTHOR

LARRY P. ARNN IS THE PRESIDENT OF HILLSDALE COLLEGE, where he also serves as a professor of politics and history and teaches courses on Aristotle, Winston Churchill, and the American Constitution. He received his B.A. from Arkansas State University, and his M.A. and Ph.D. in Government from the Claremont Graduate School. He also studied at the London School of Economics and Oxford University. While in England, he also served as director of research for Martin Gilbert, now Sir Martin, the official biographer of Winston Churchill. He has served as president of the Claremont Institute.

Dr. Arnn has been published widely in national newspapers, magazines and periodicals on issues of public policy, history and political theory, and he is the author of *Liberty and Learning: The Evolution of American Education*, published by Hillsdale College Press in 2004. He and his wife, Penny, have four children.